GEOMETRIC COLORING BOOK

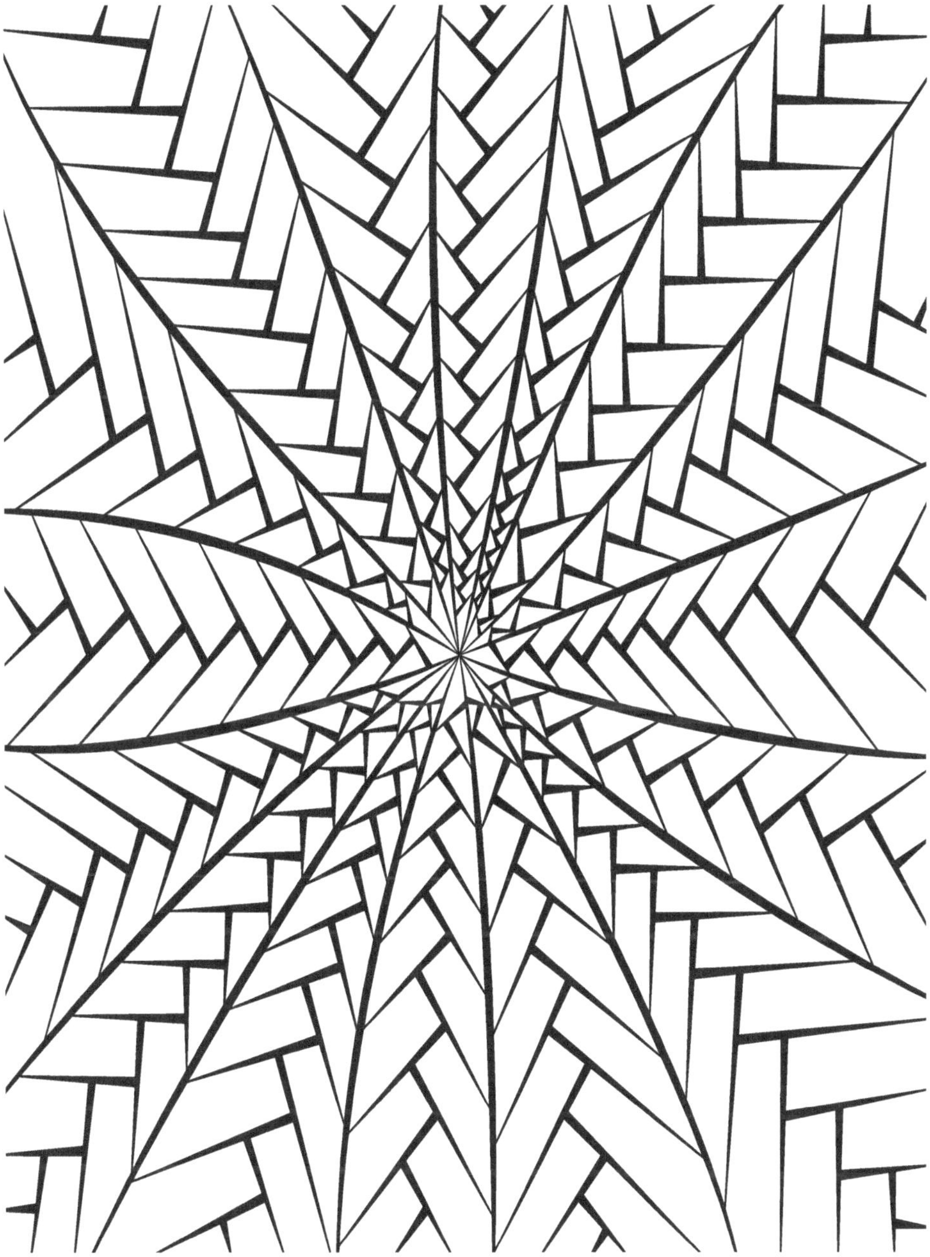

- RUSS FOCUS -

ISBN-13: 978-1727088540 ISBN-10: 1727088549

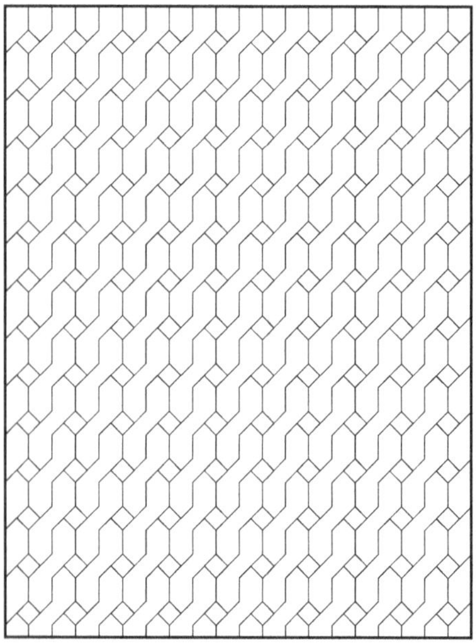

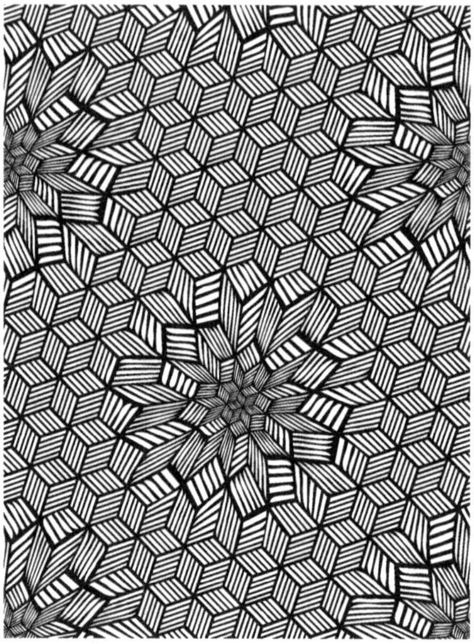

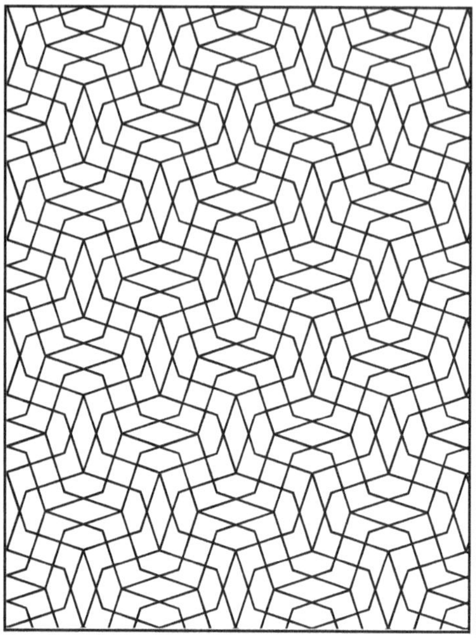

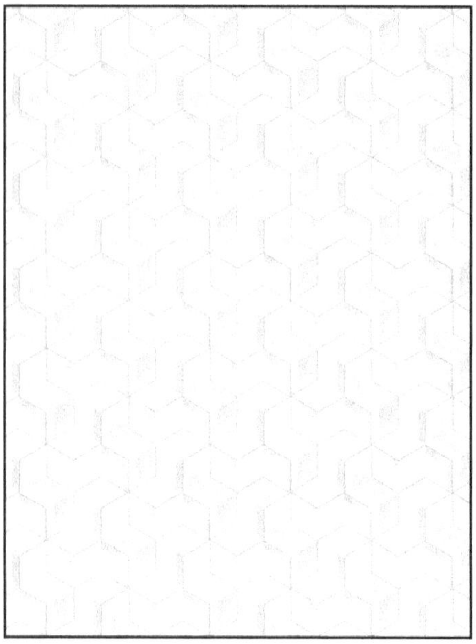

SAMPLE GEOMETRIC COLORING 17 of 50 PAGES

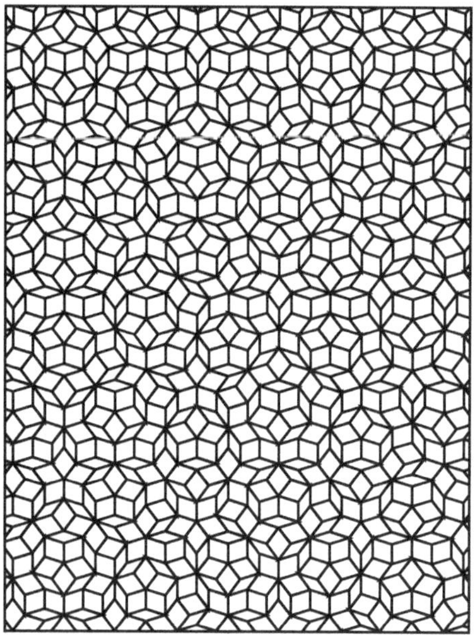

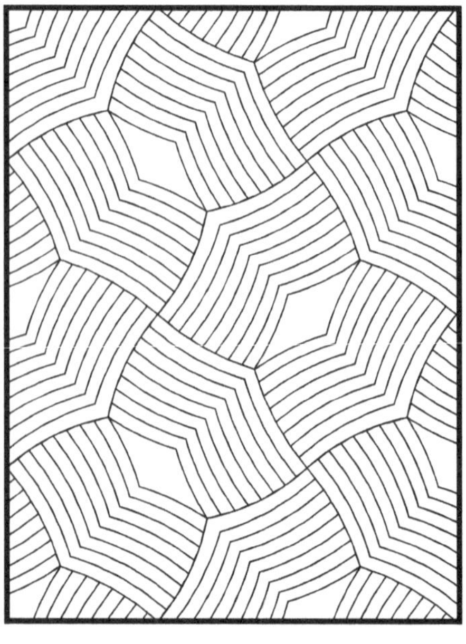

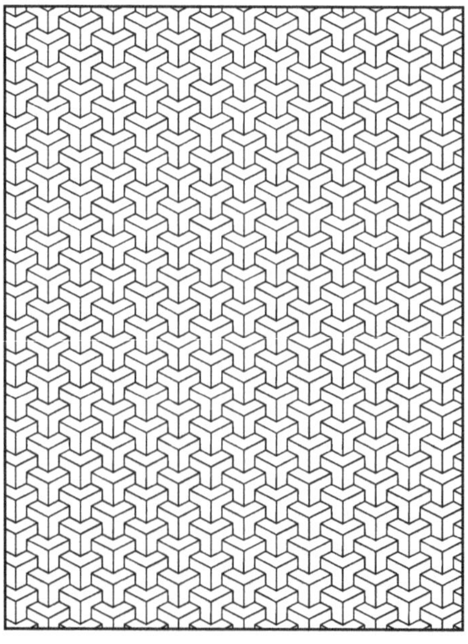

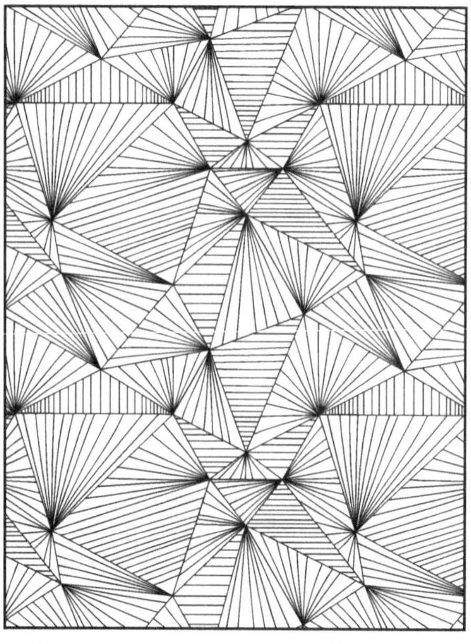

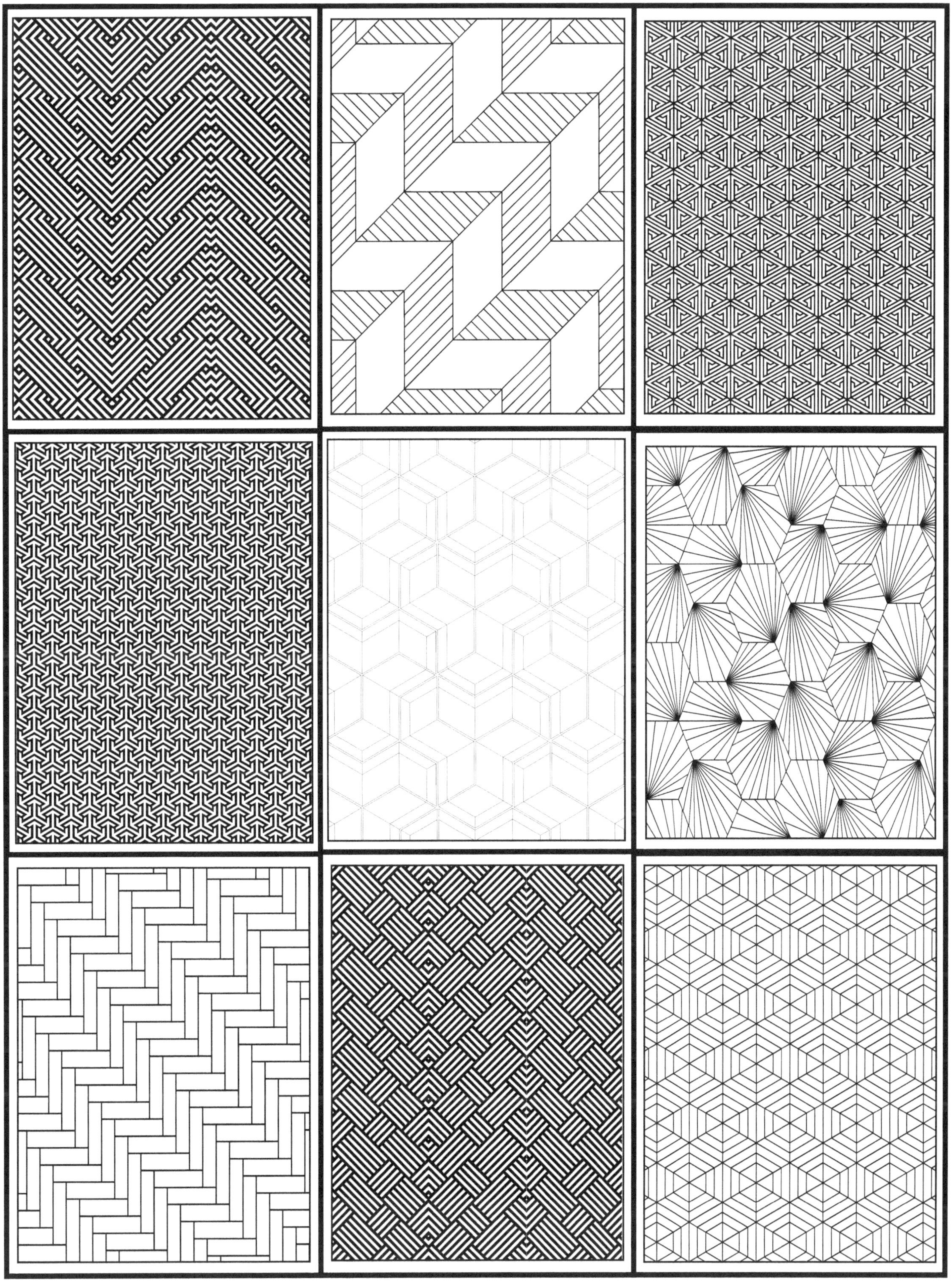

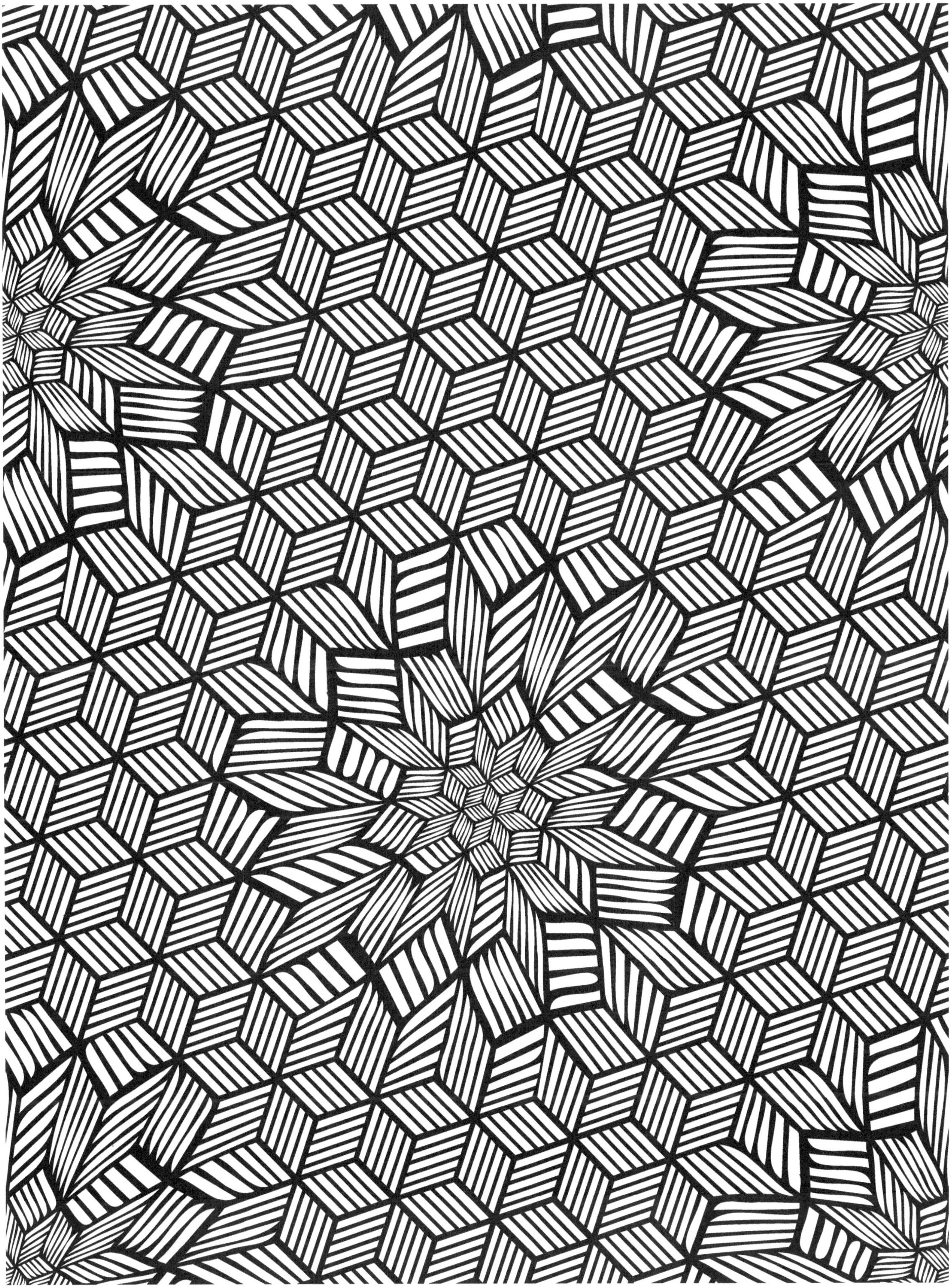

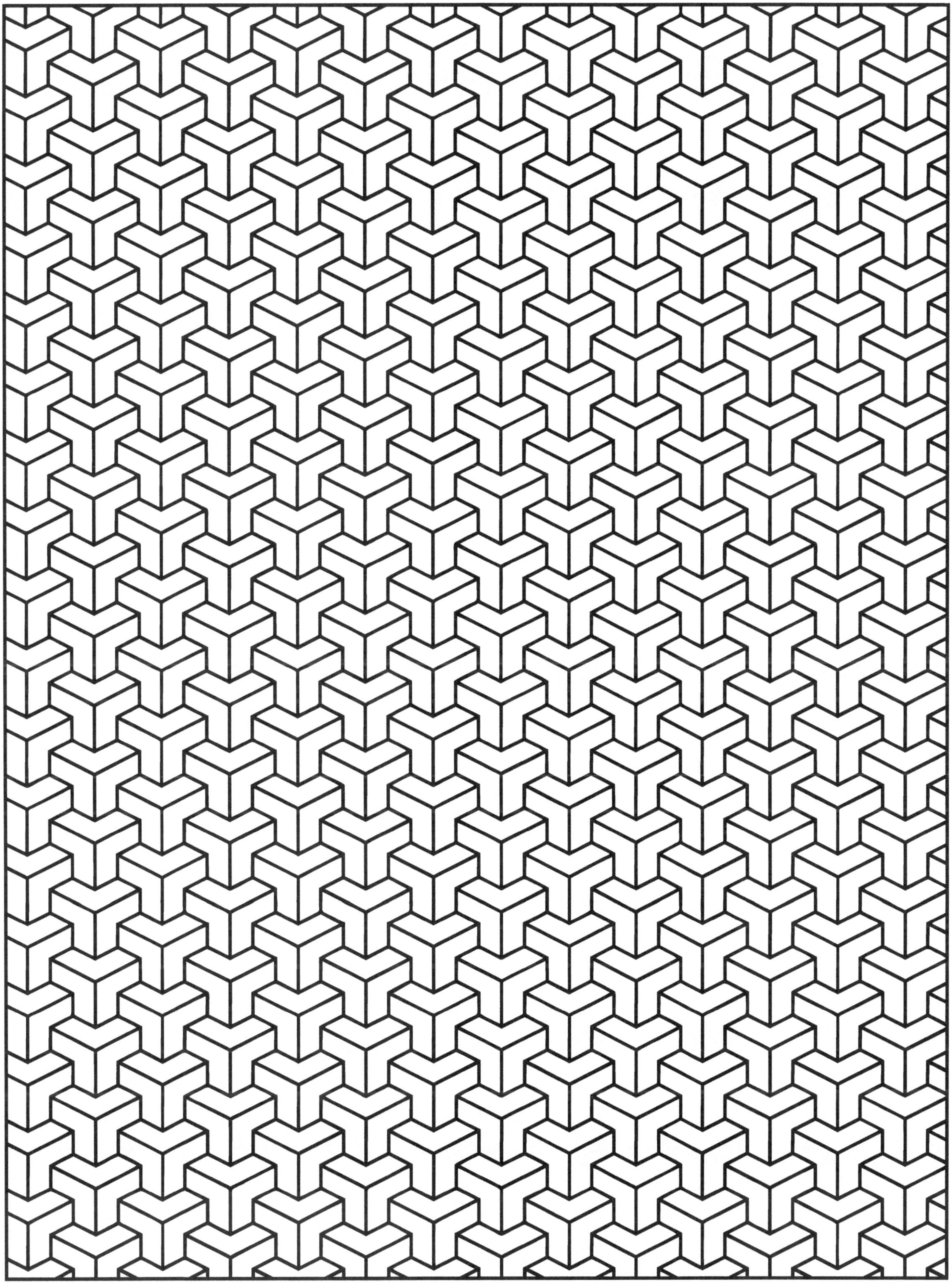

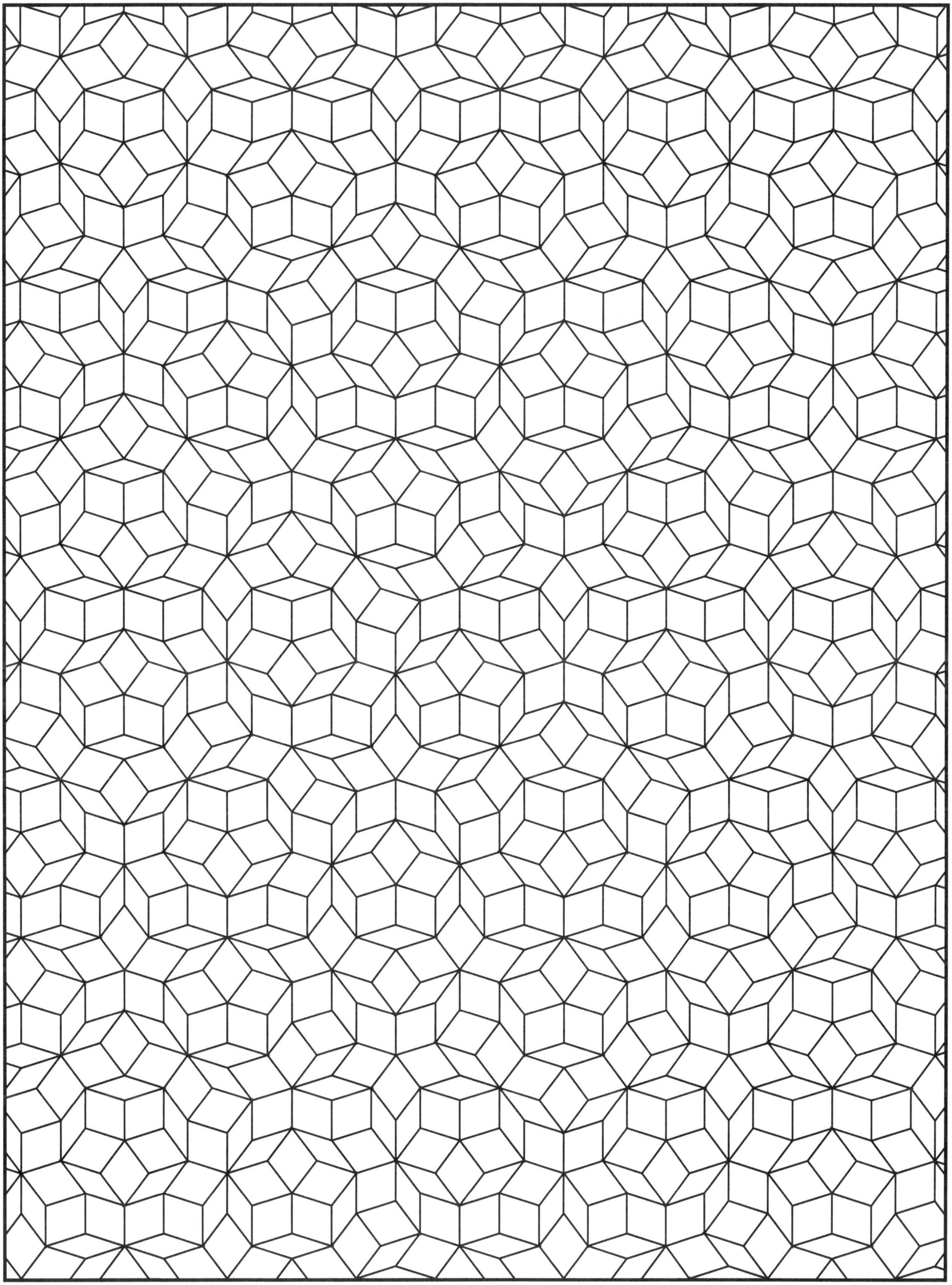

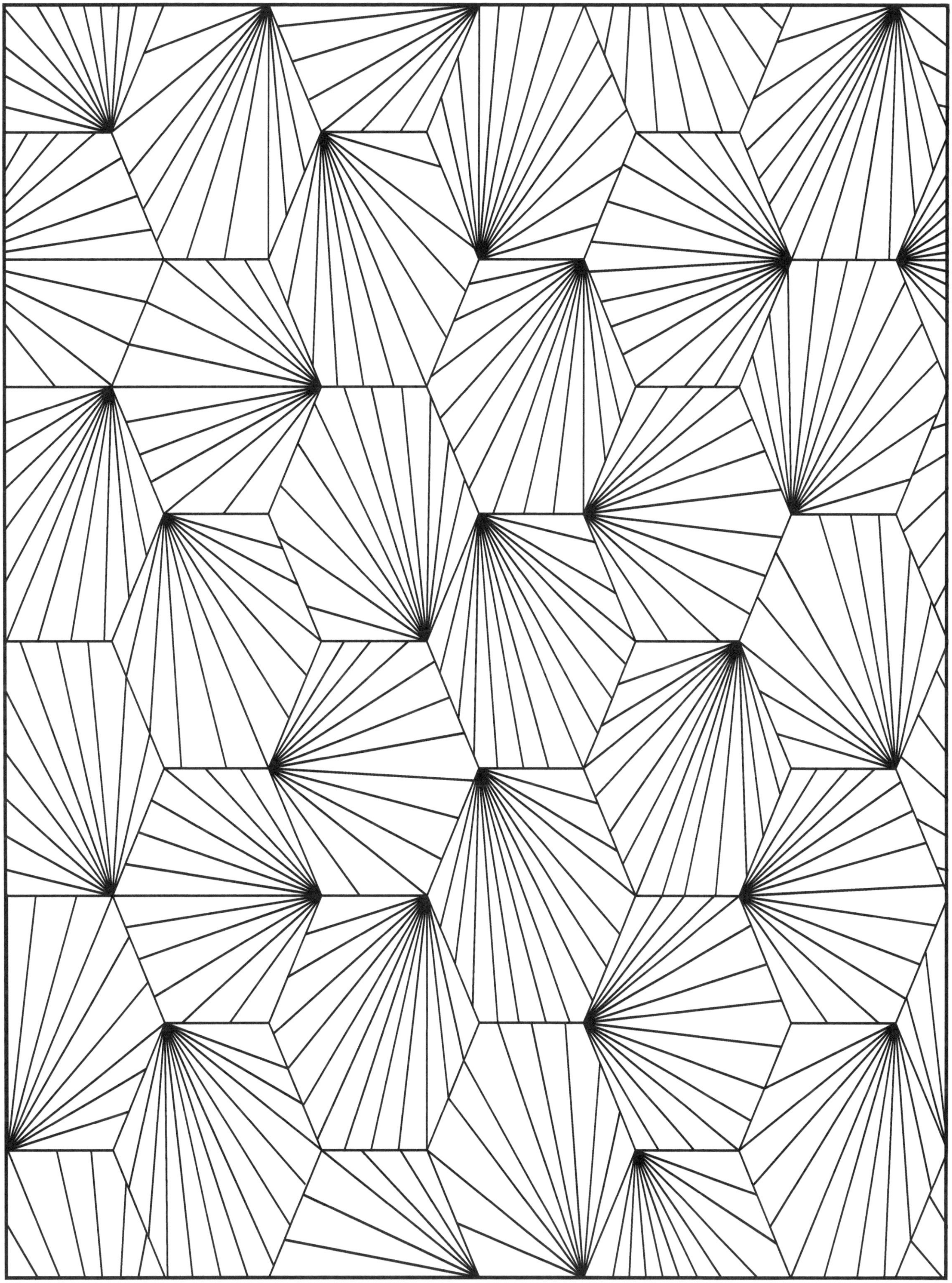

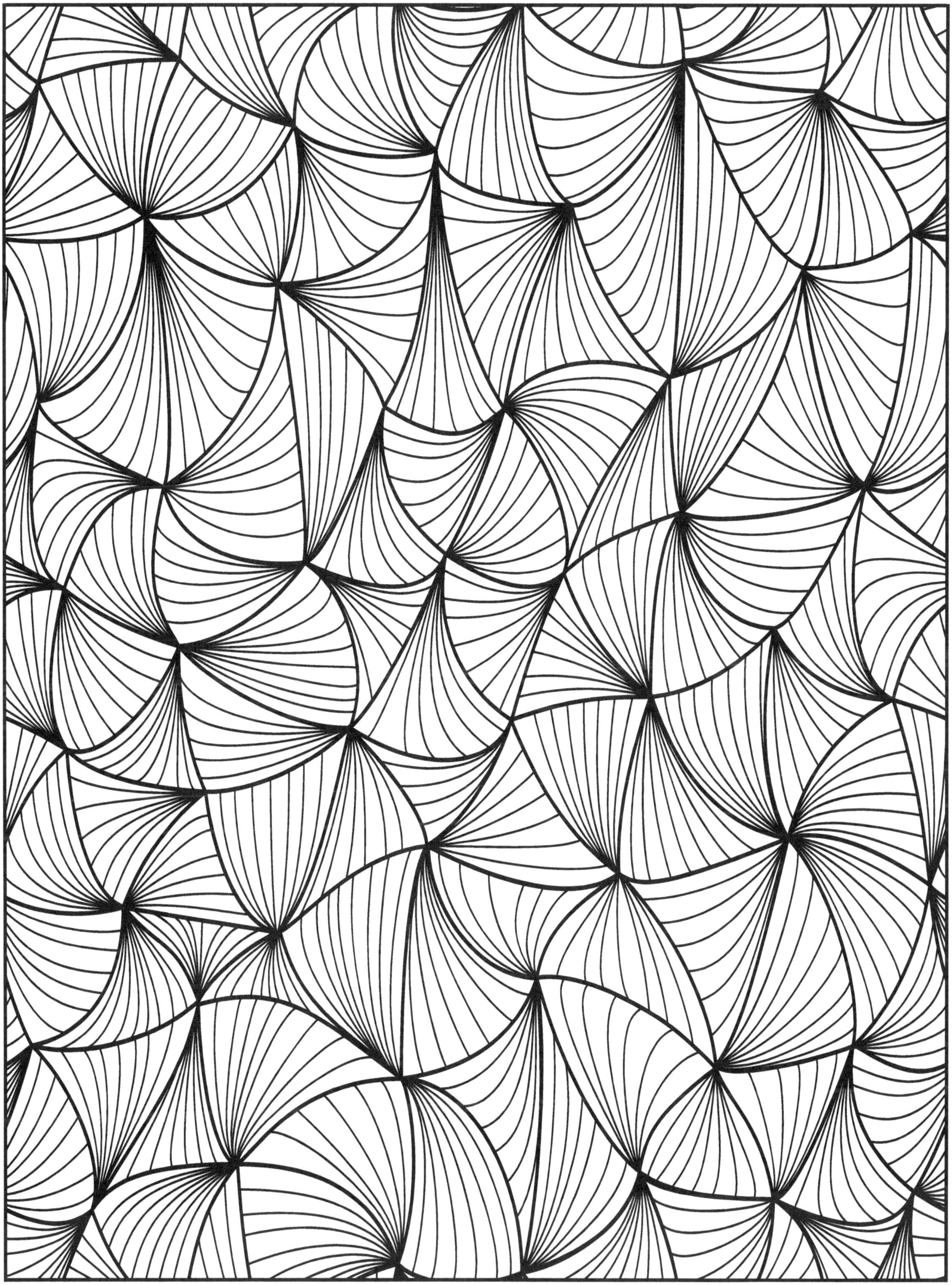

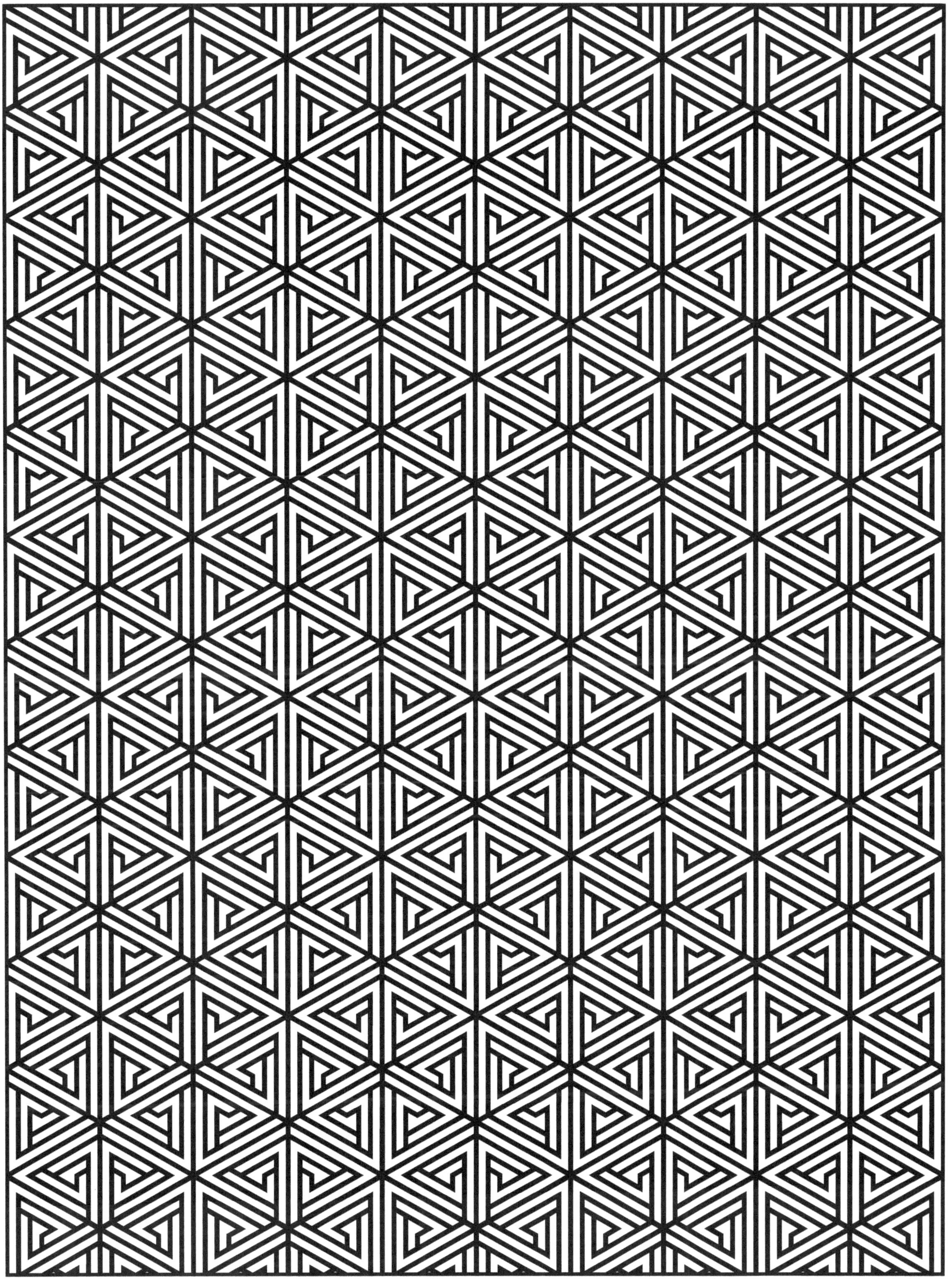

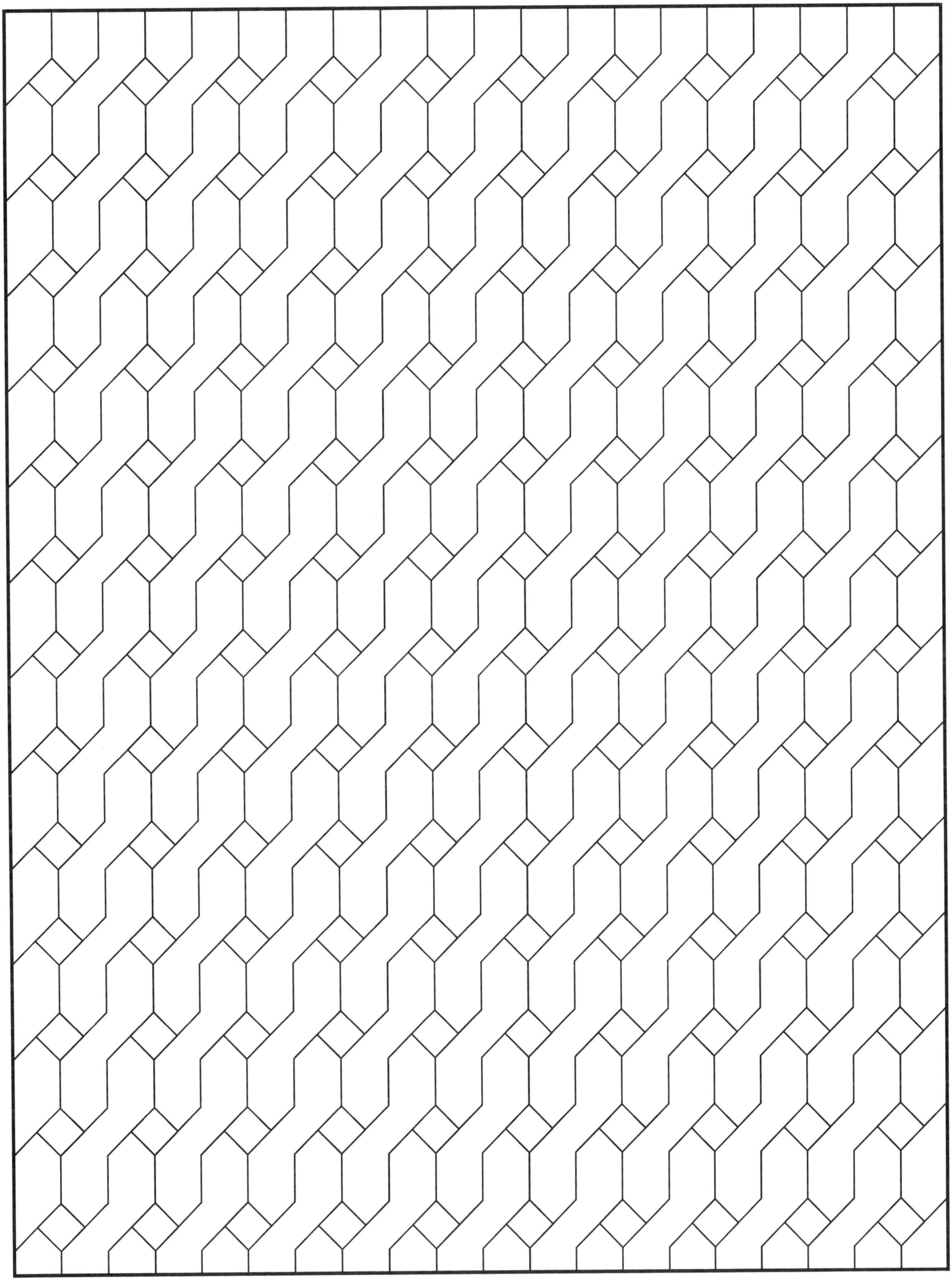

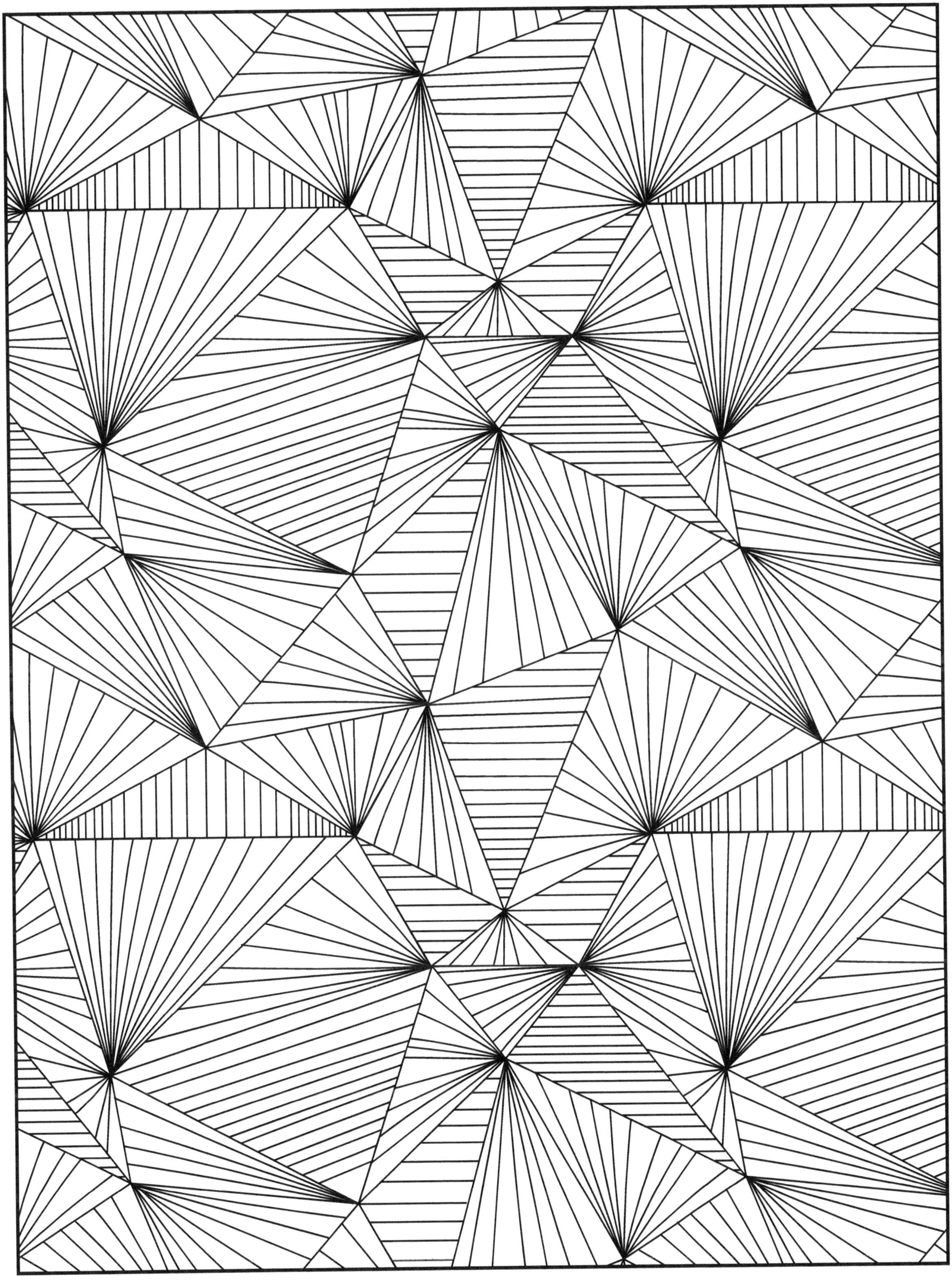

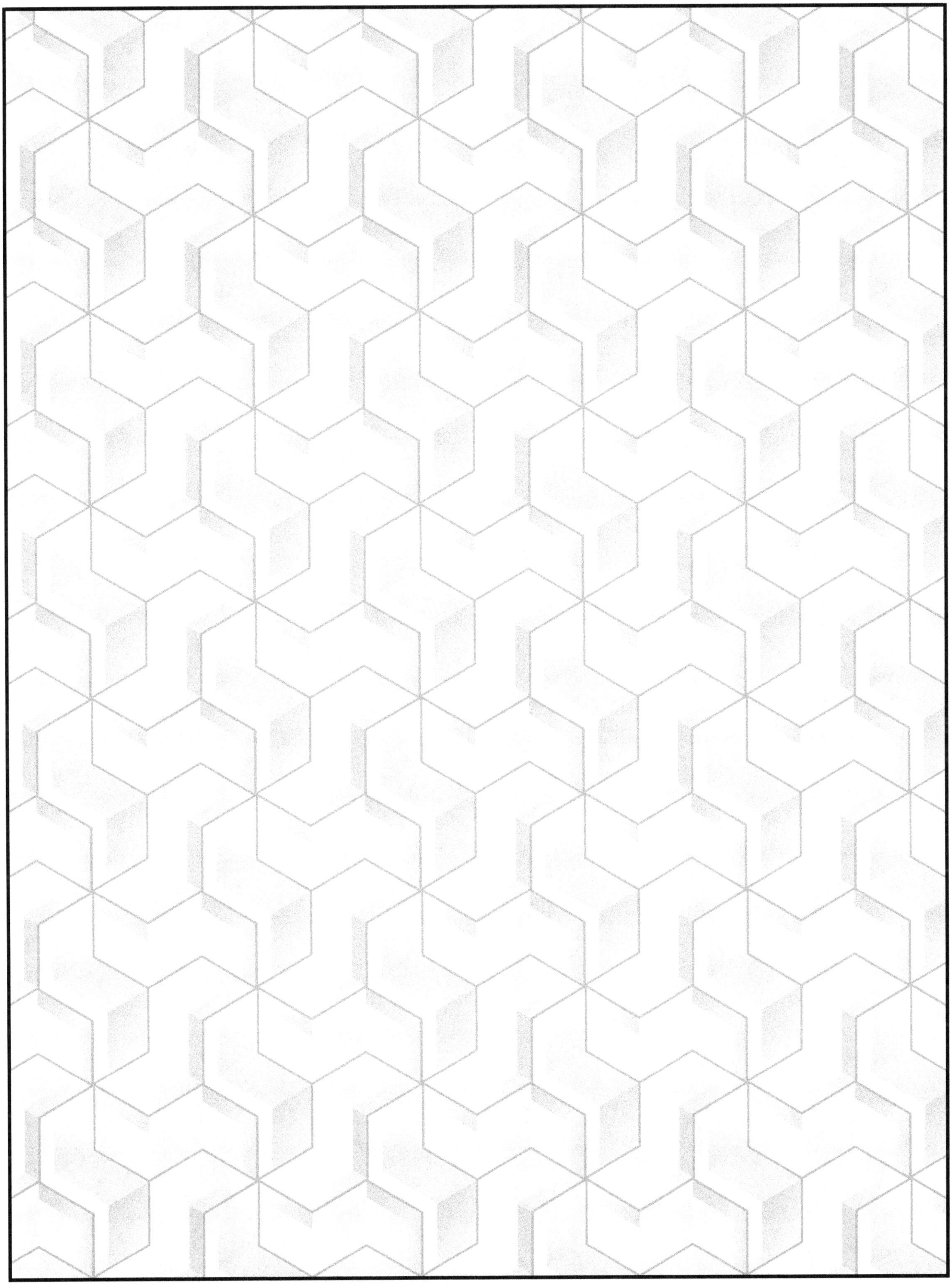

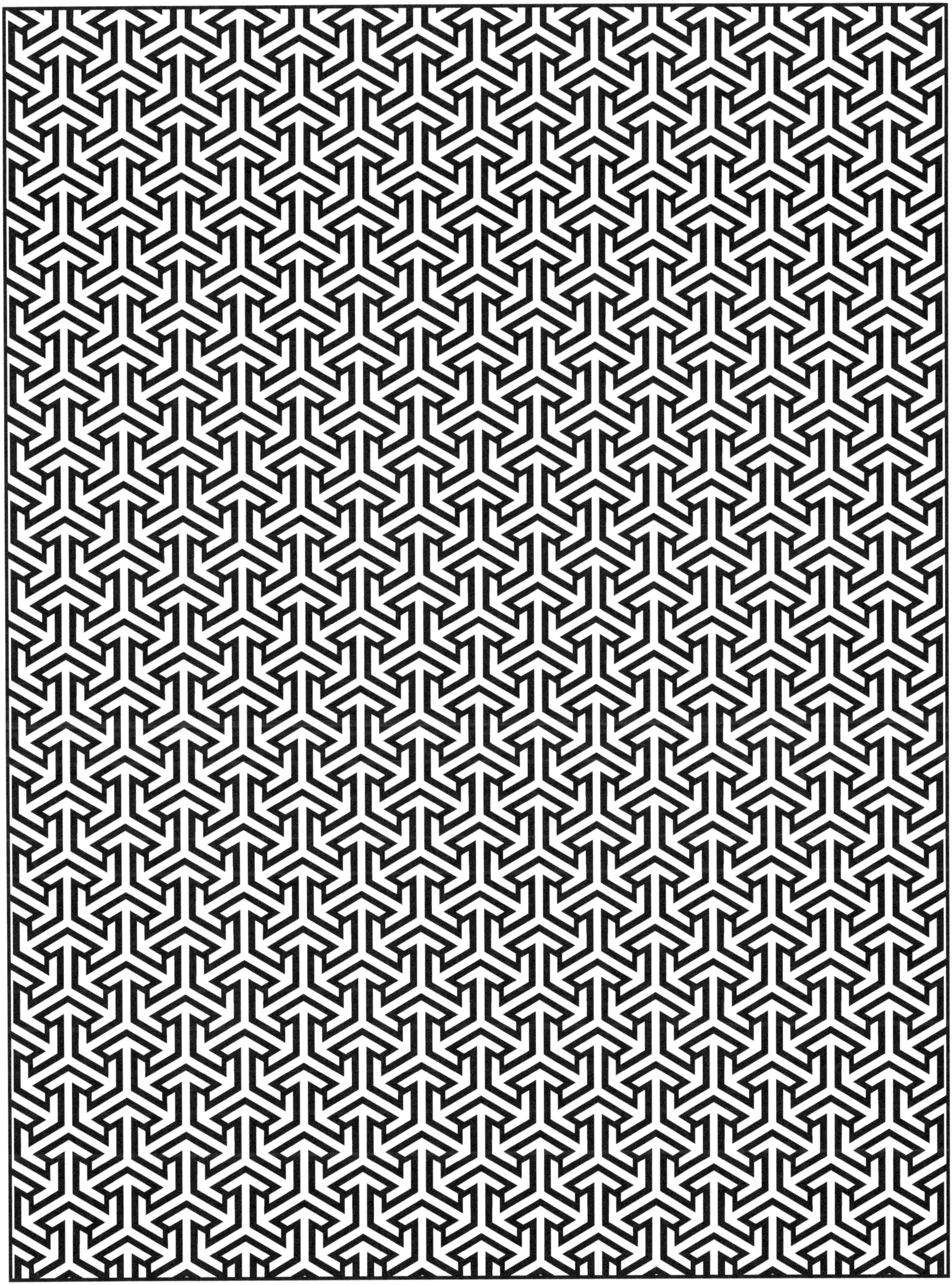

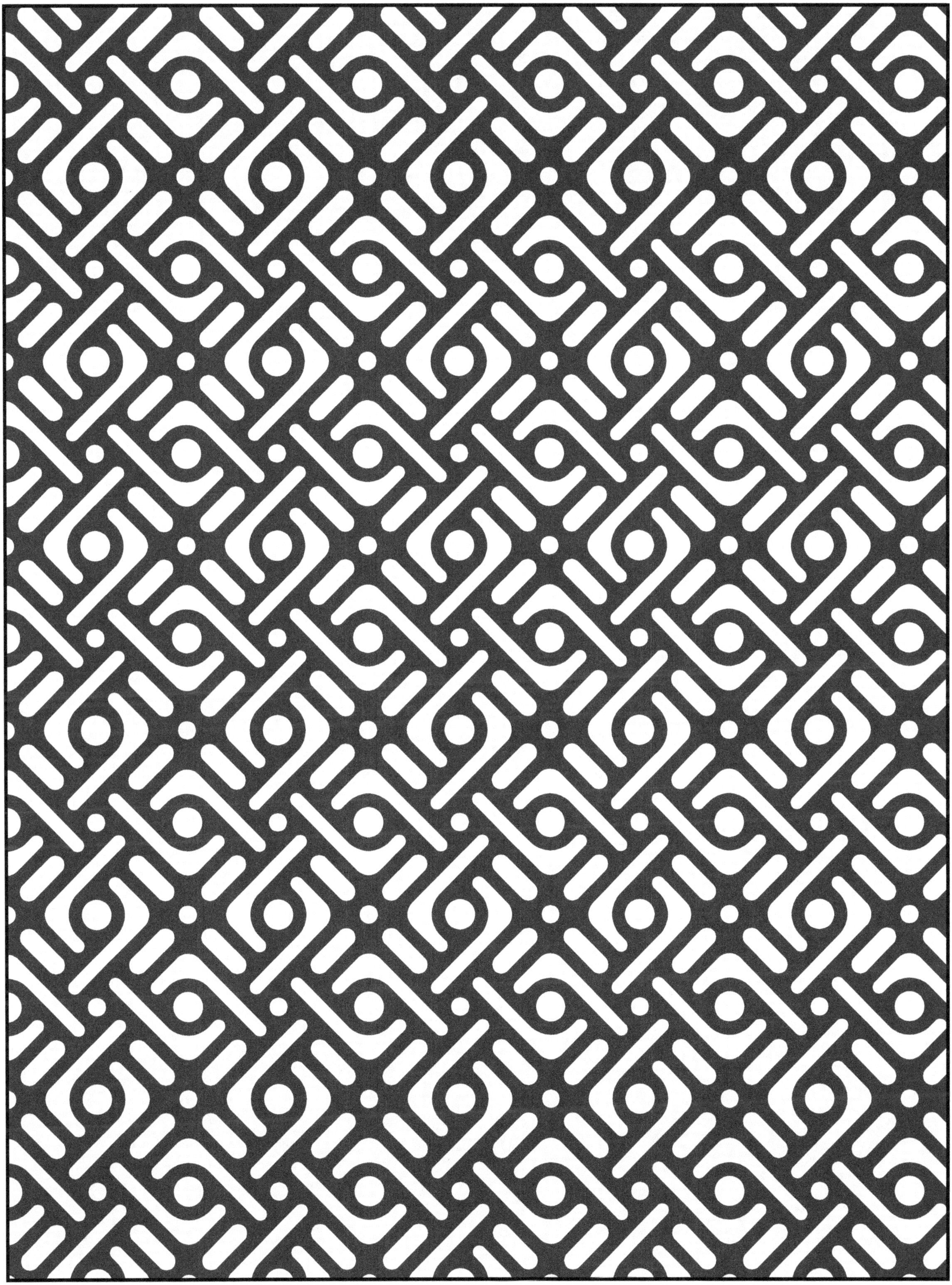

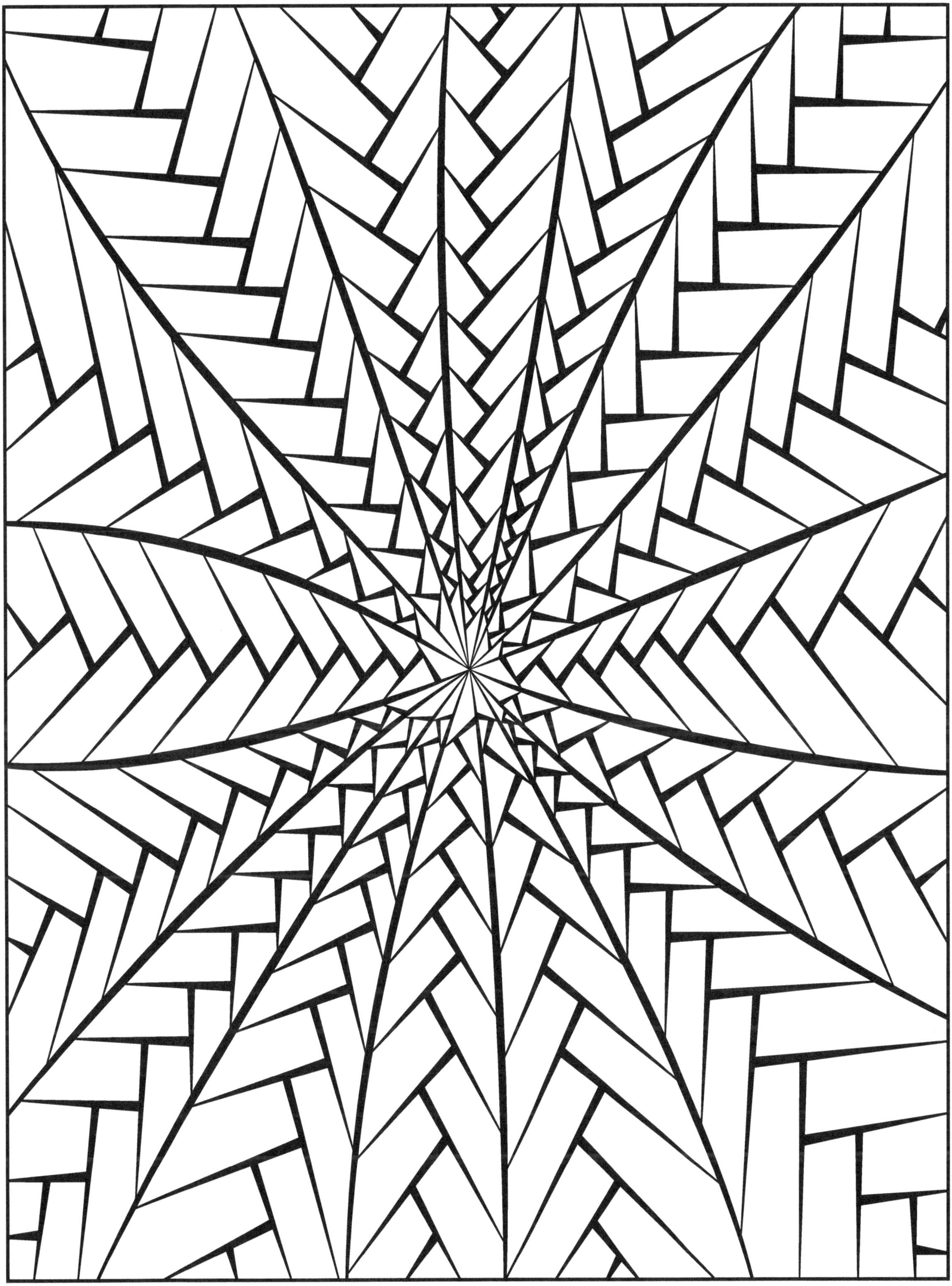

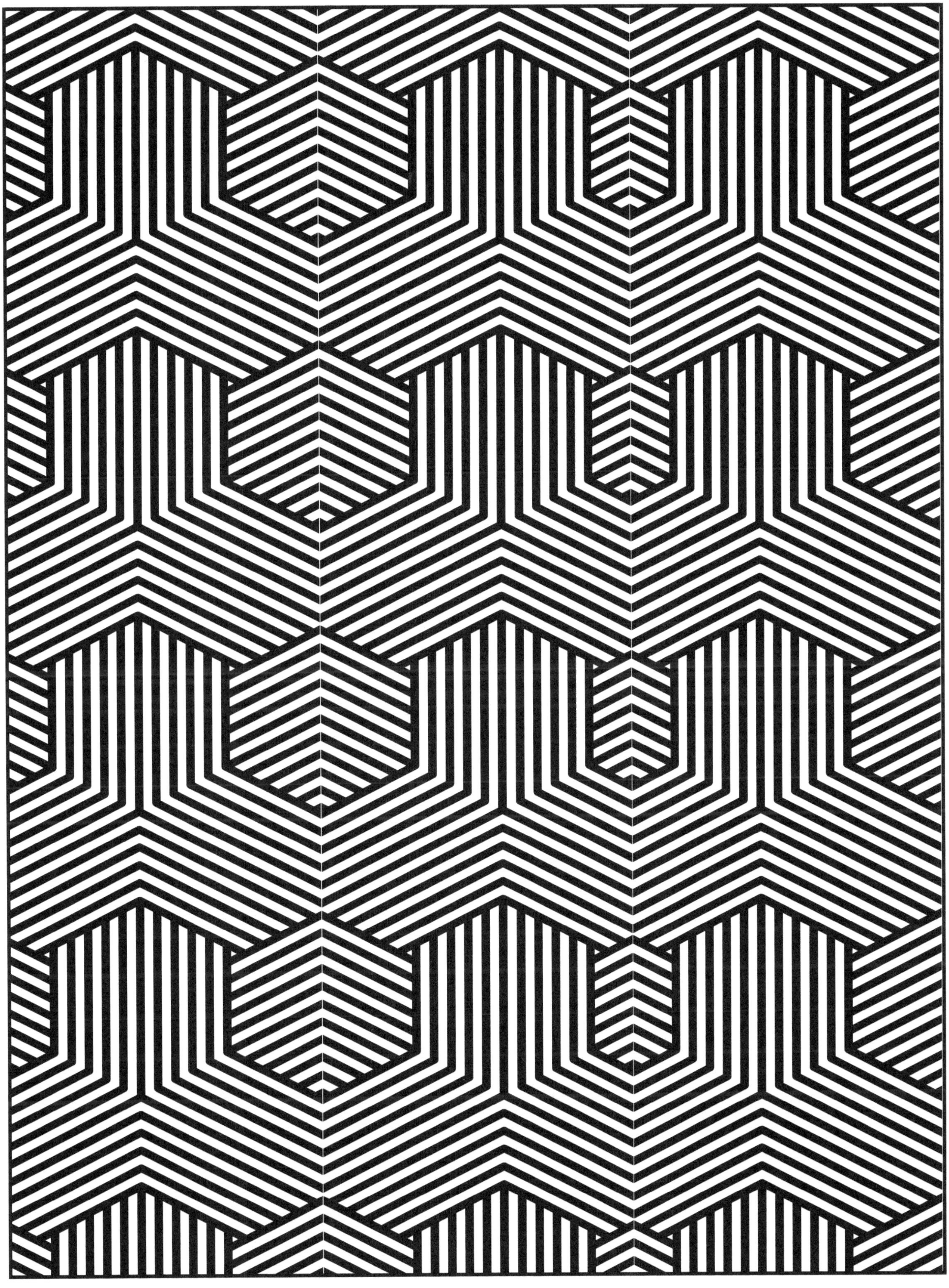

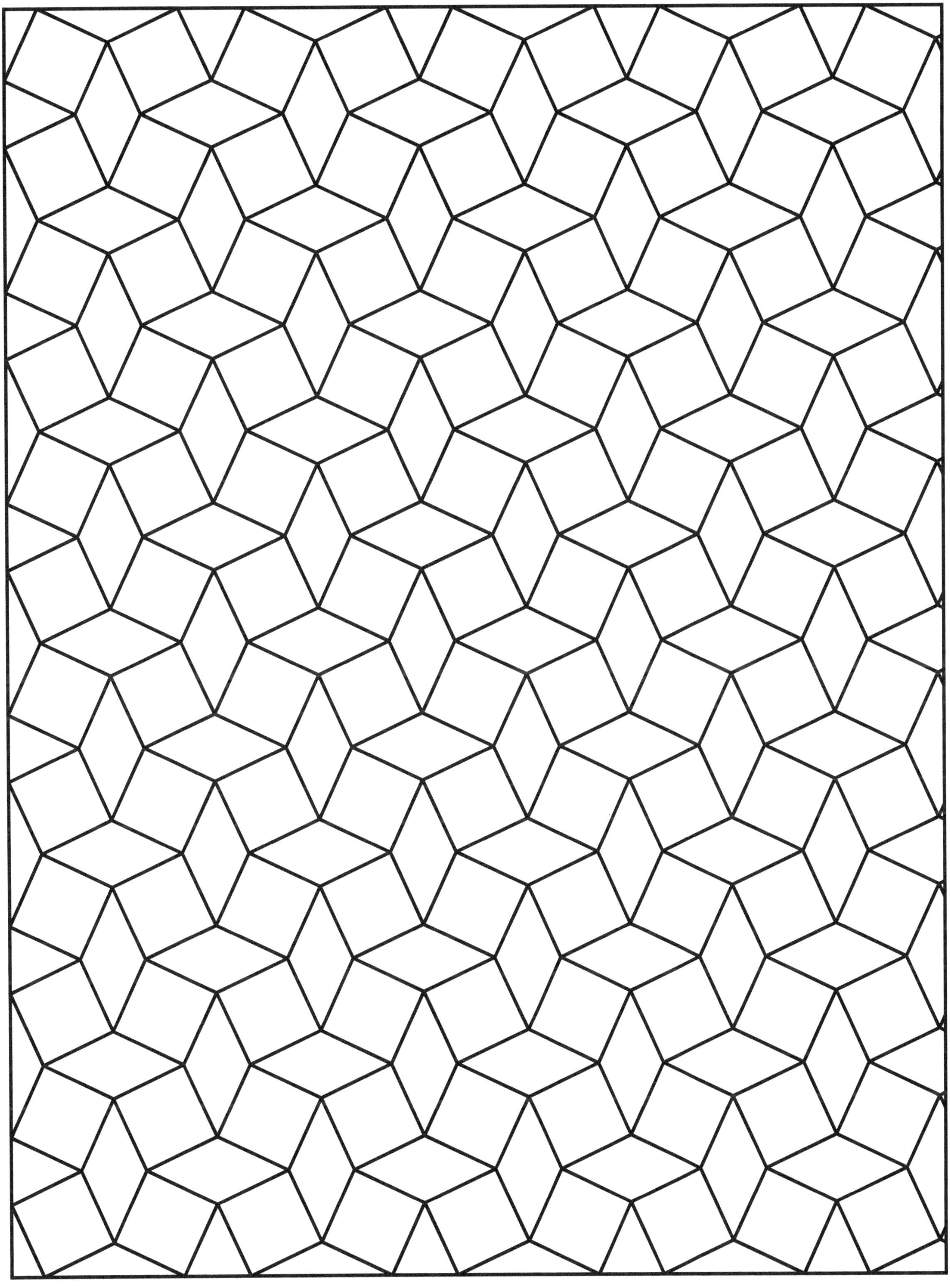

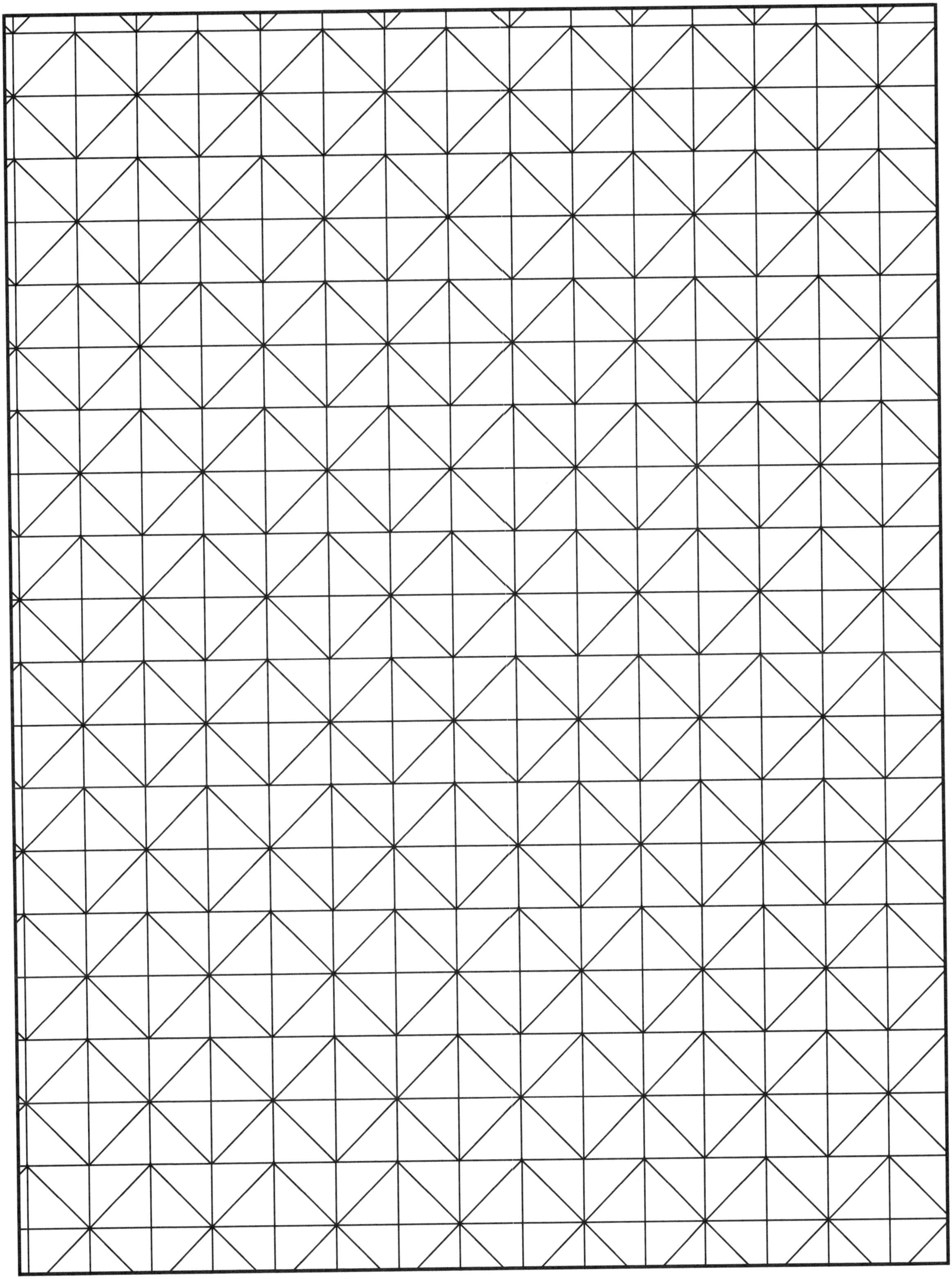

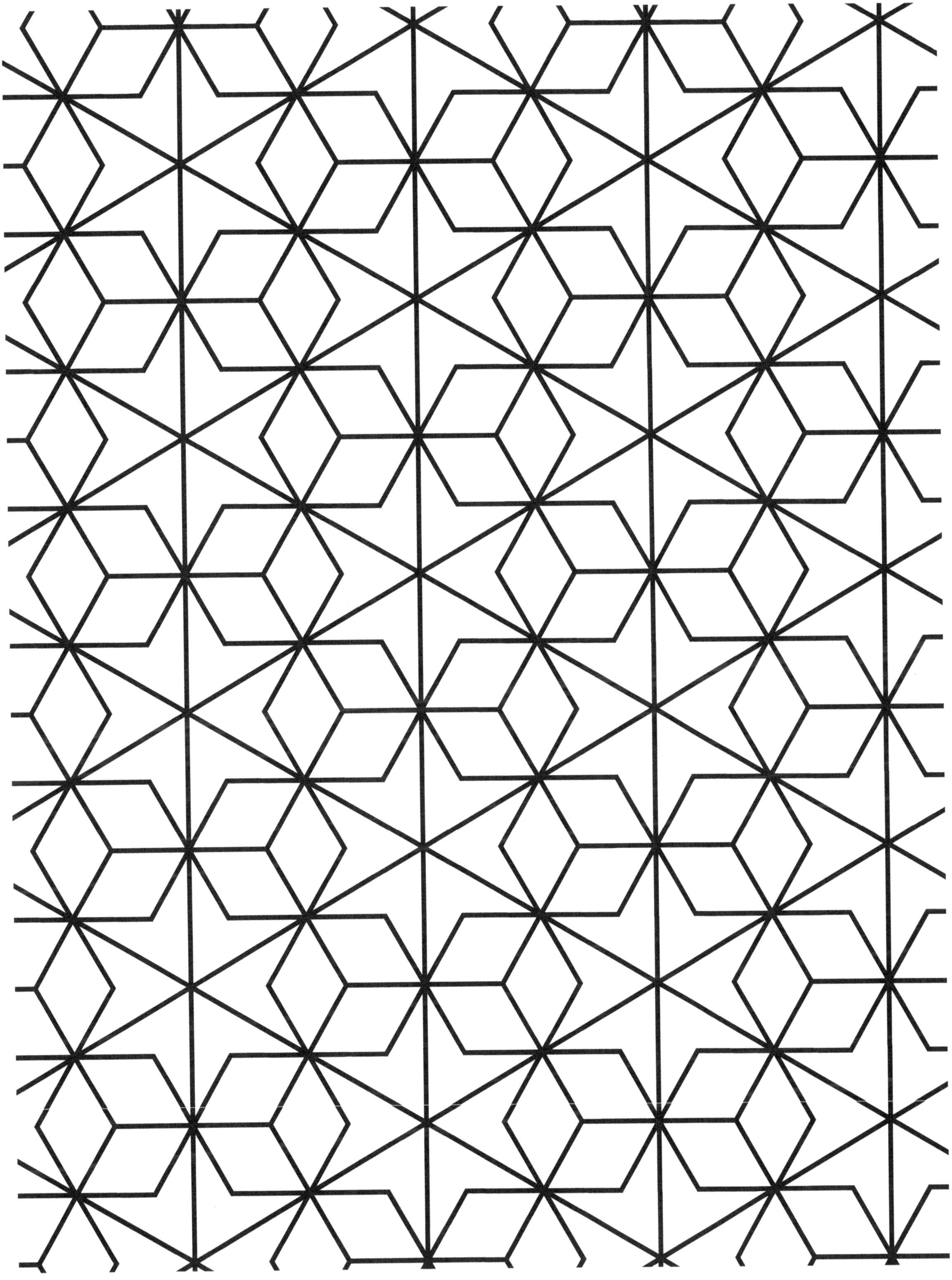

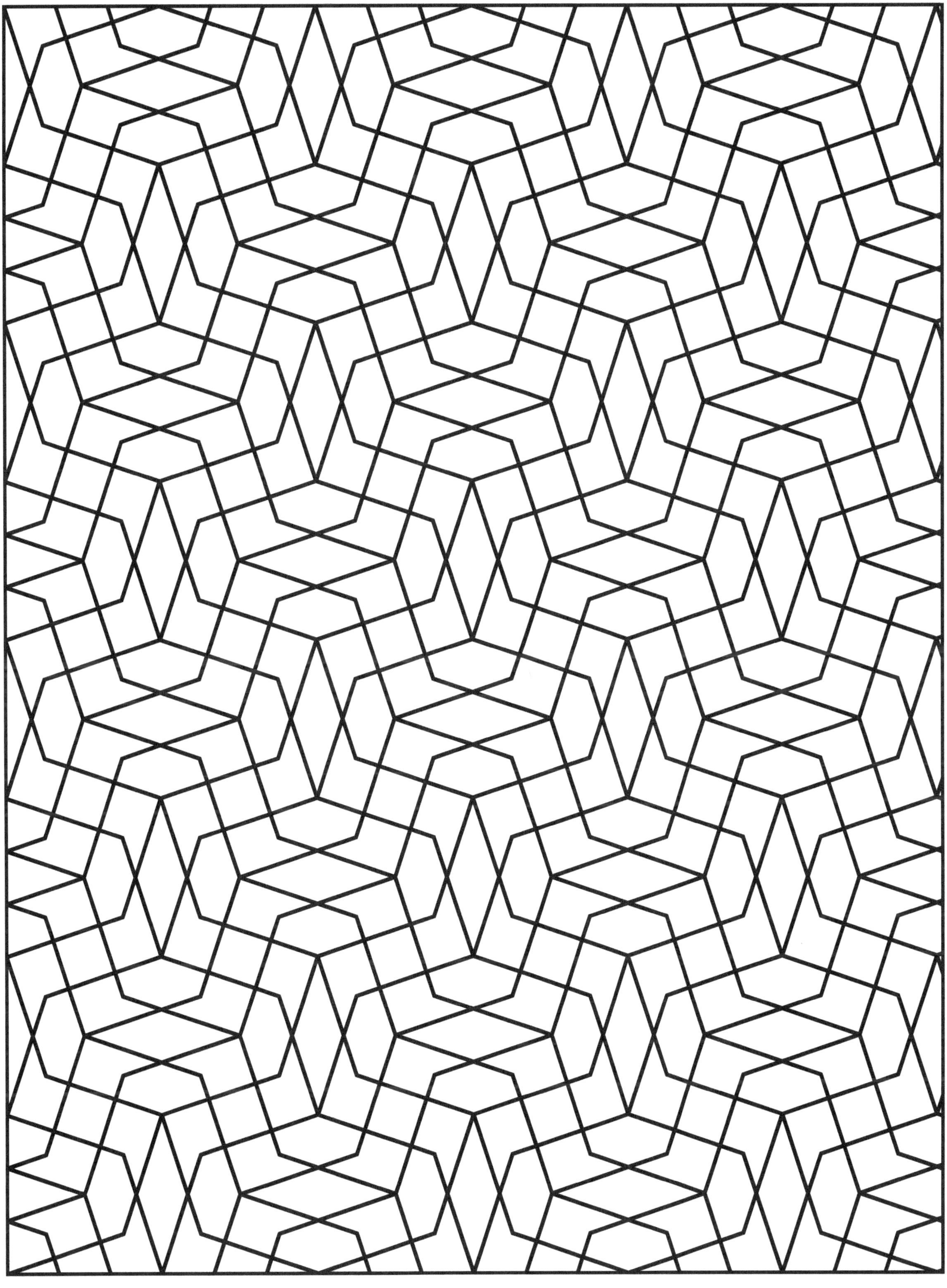

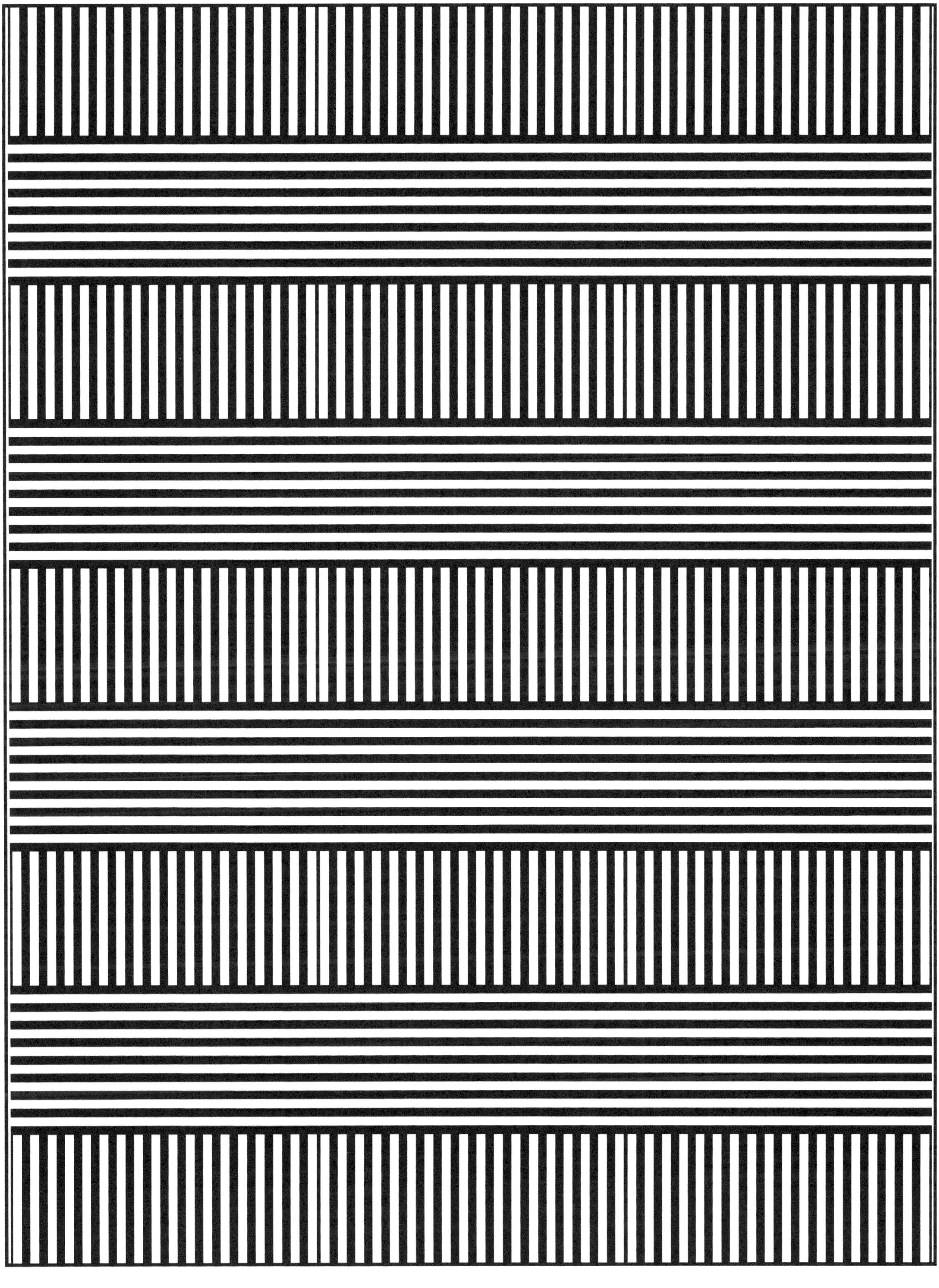

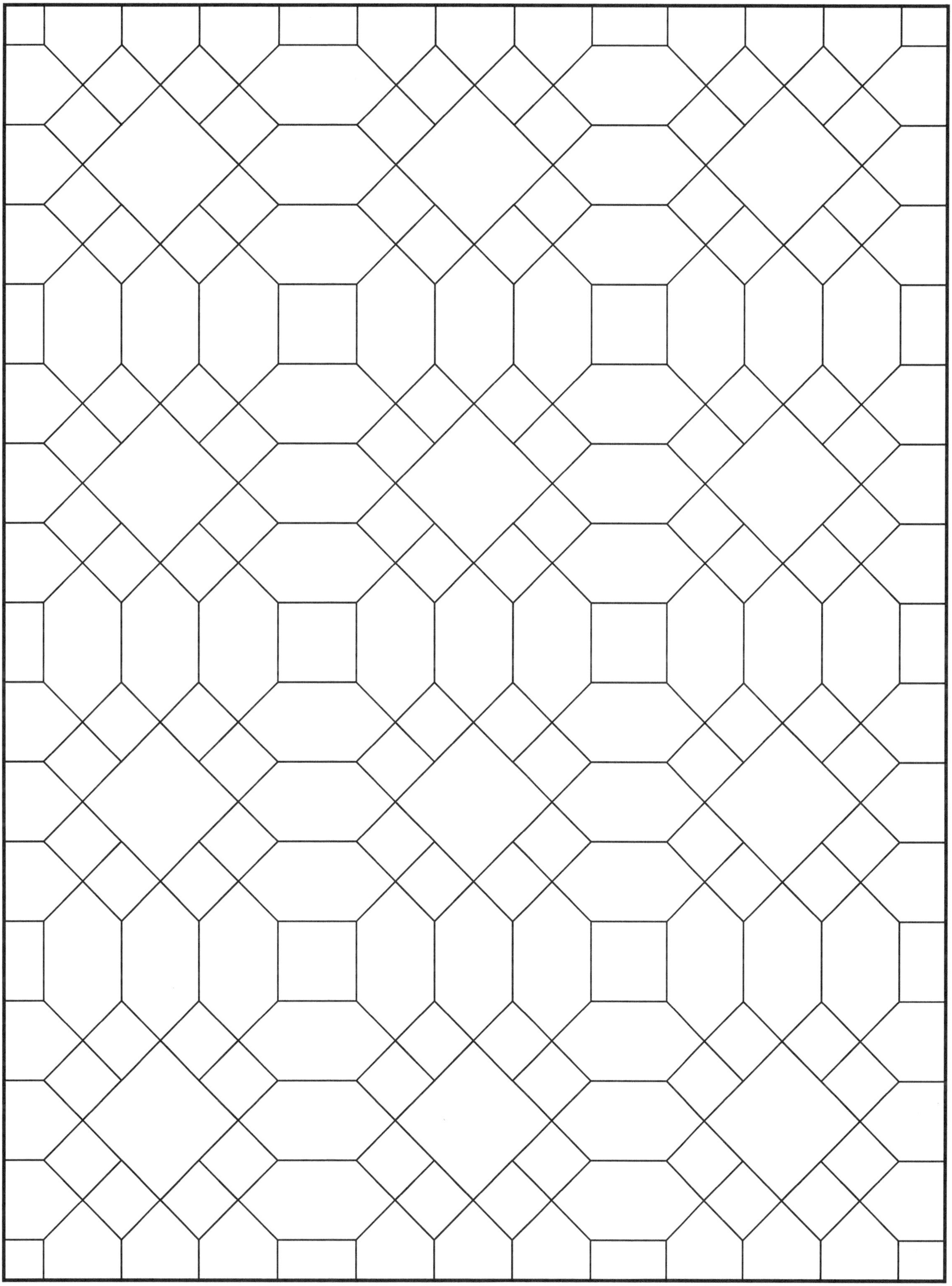

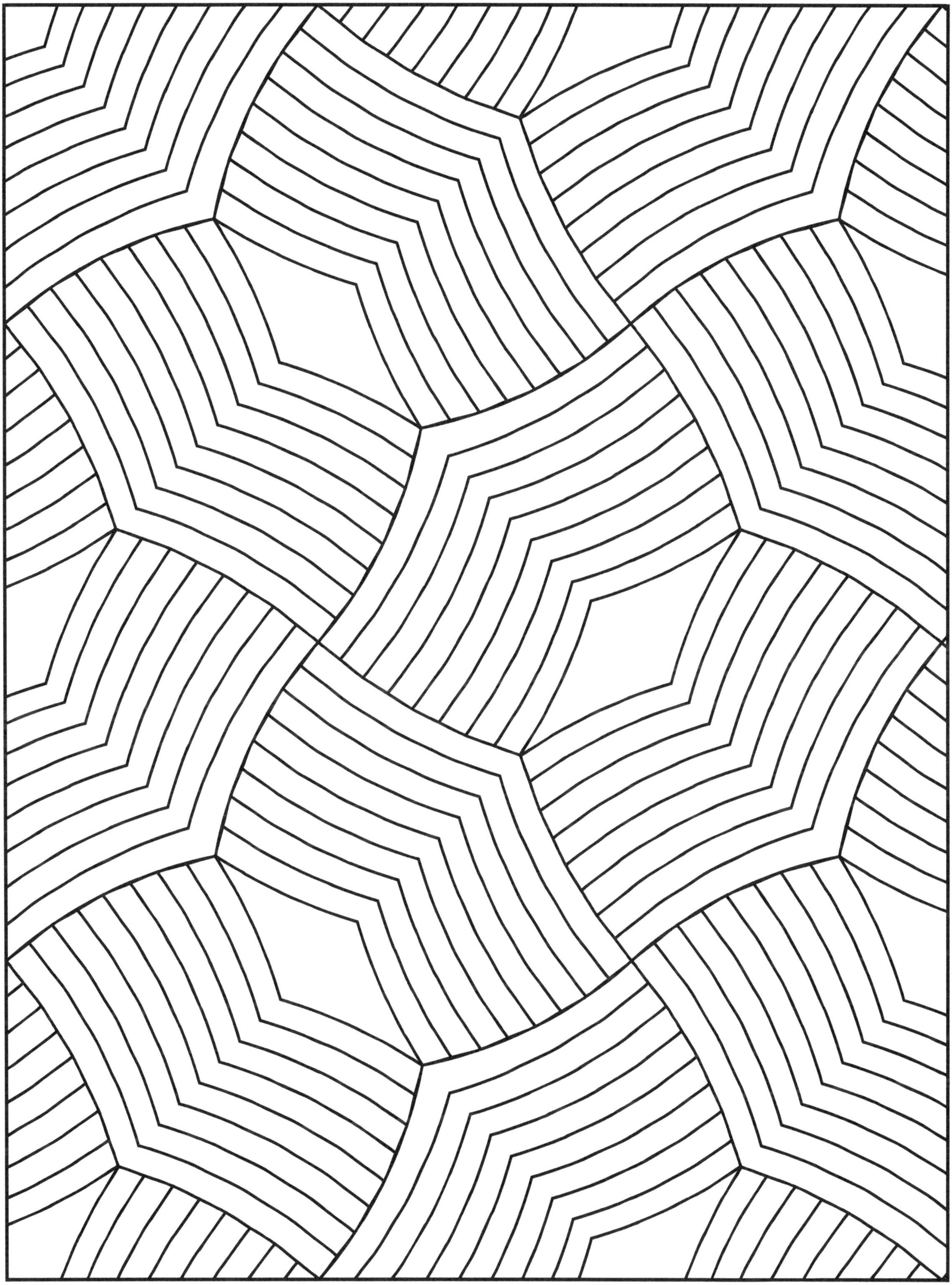

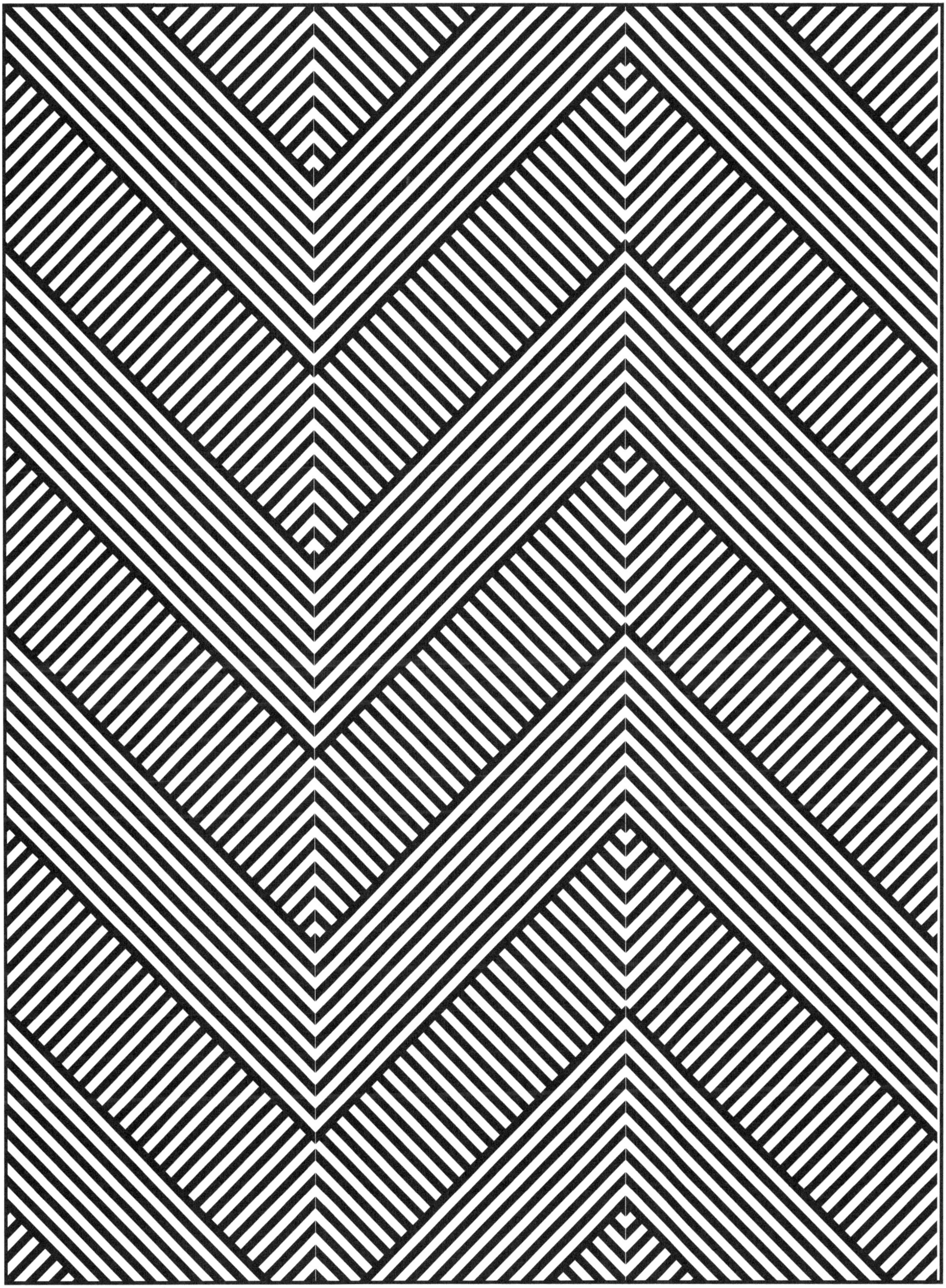

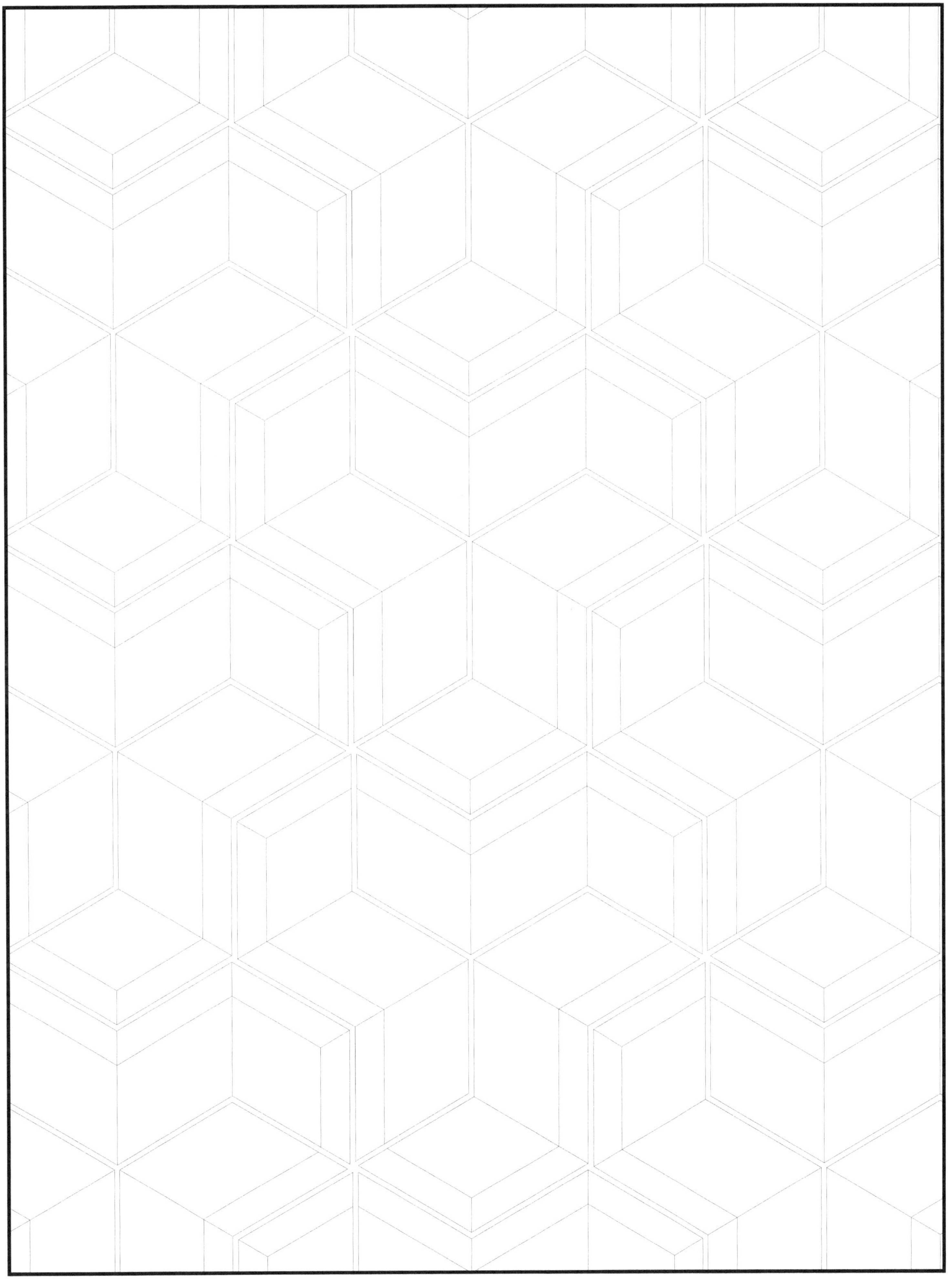

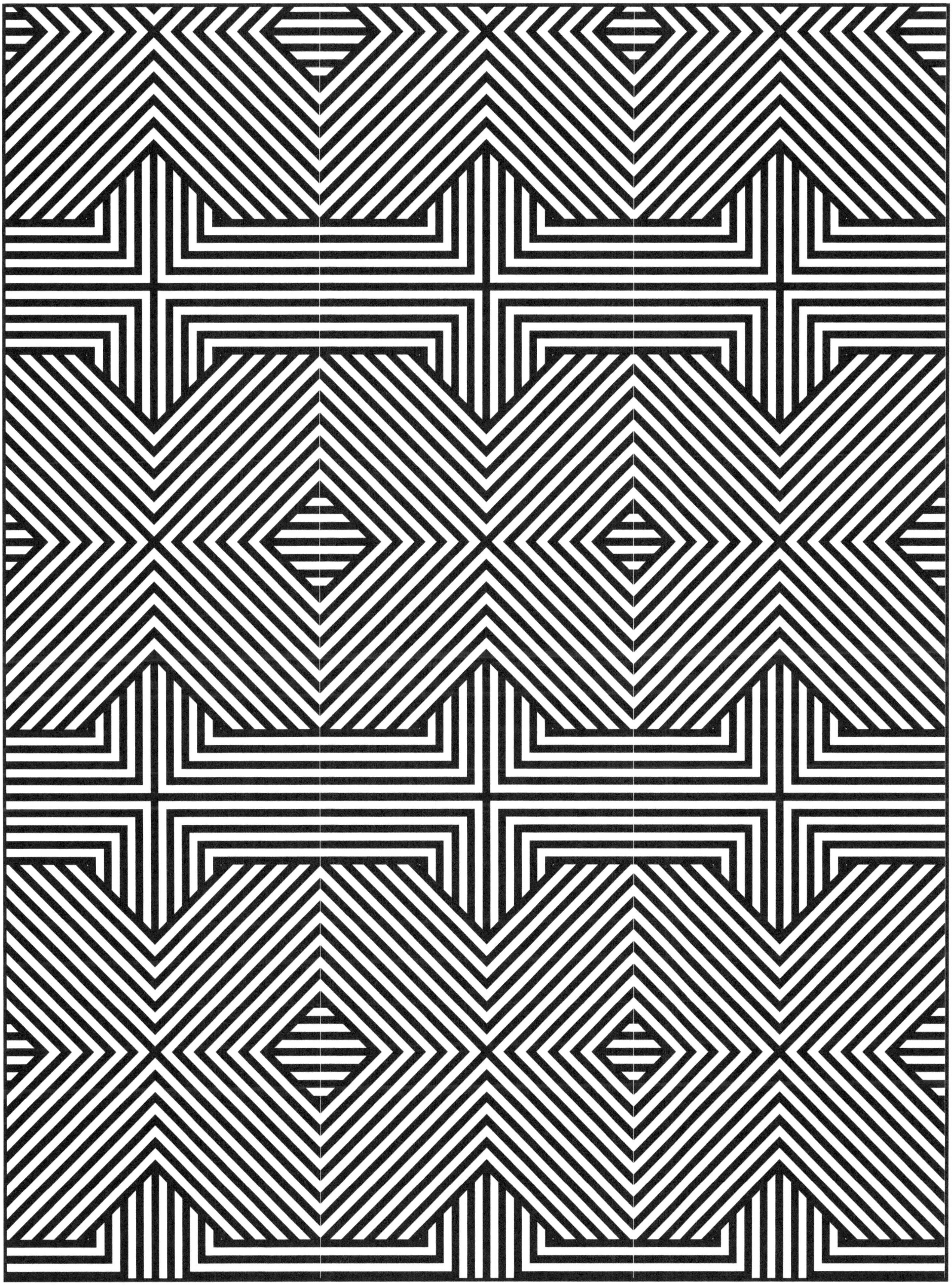

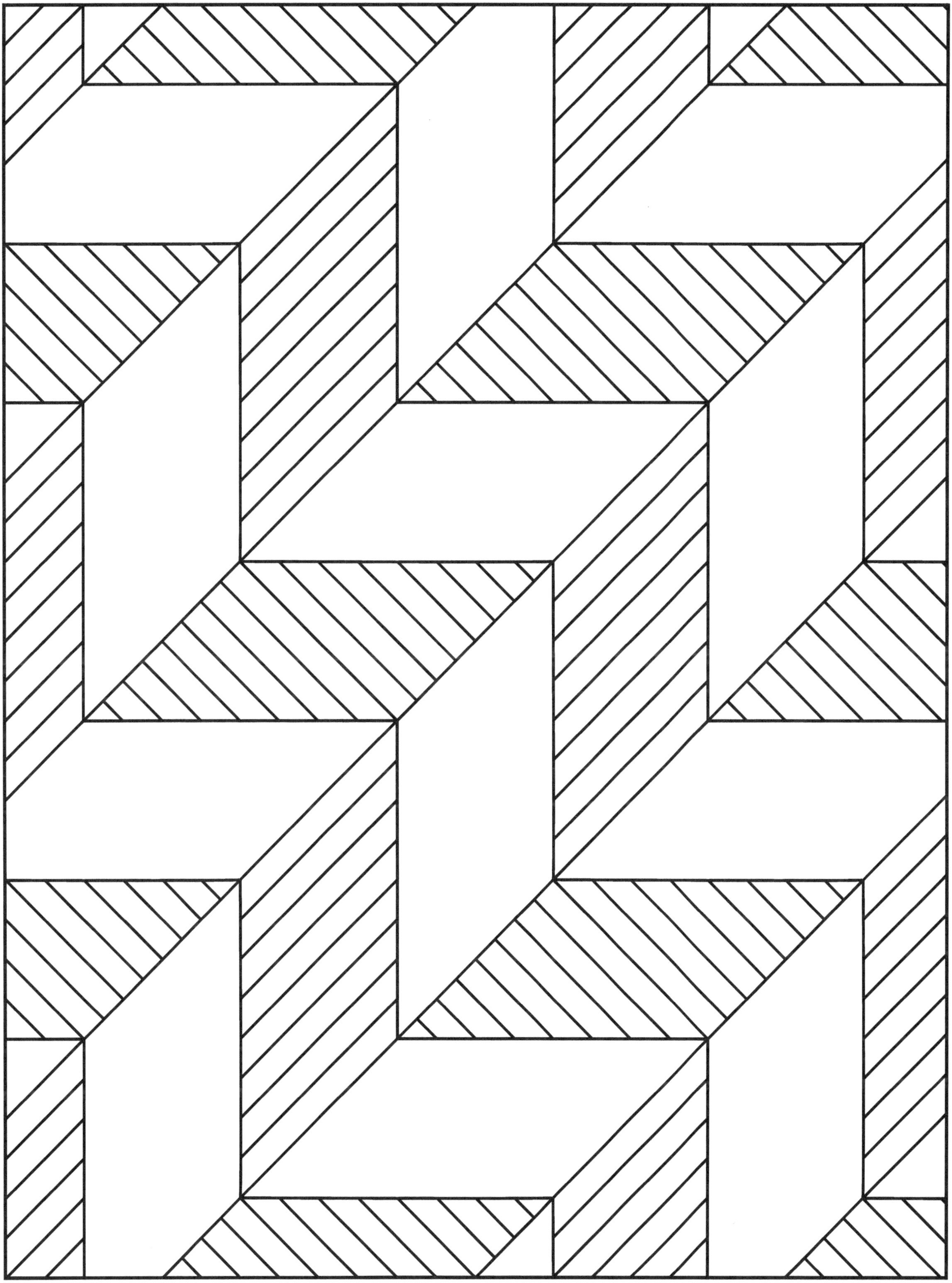

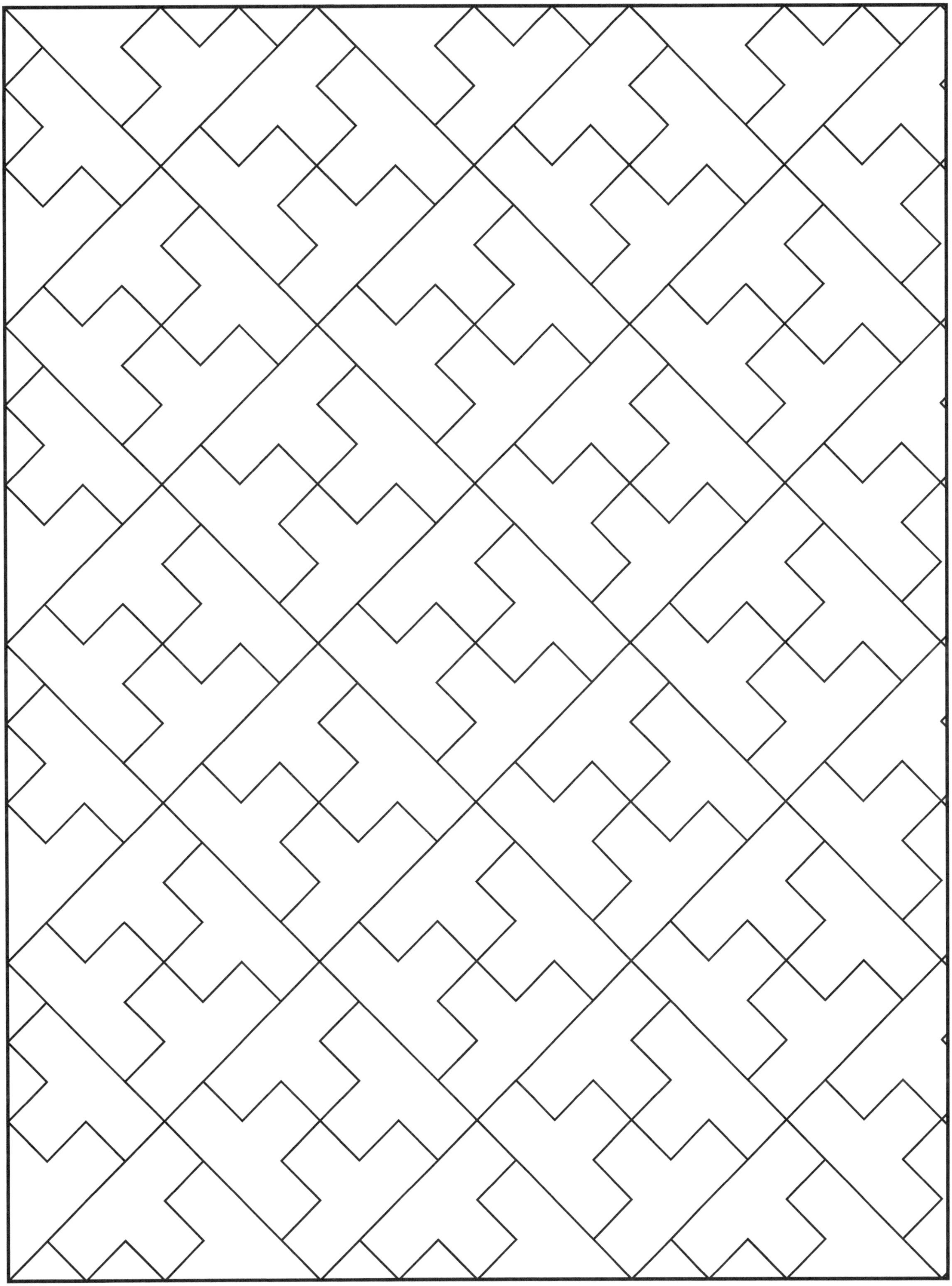

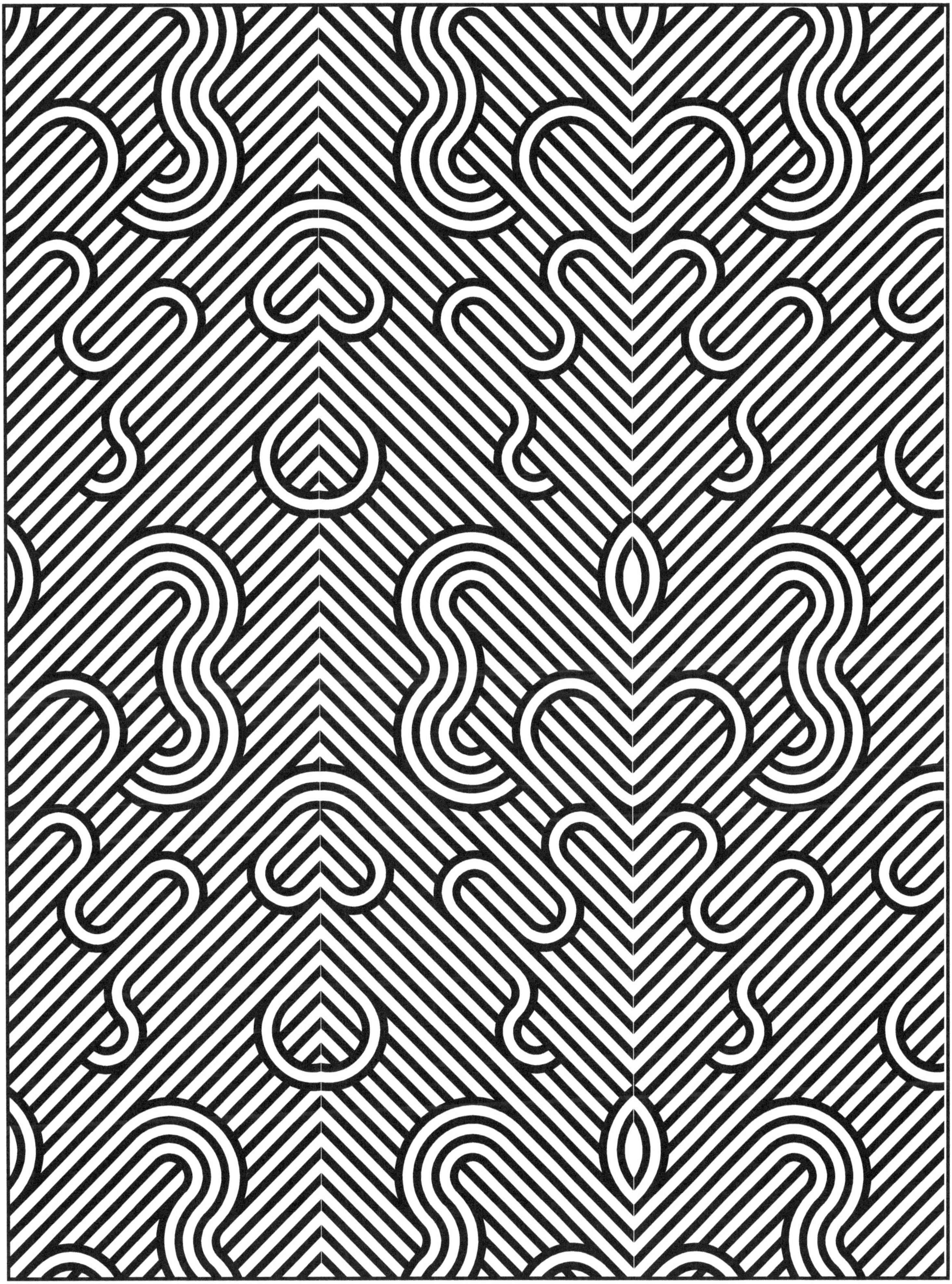

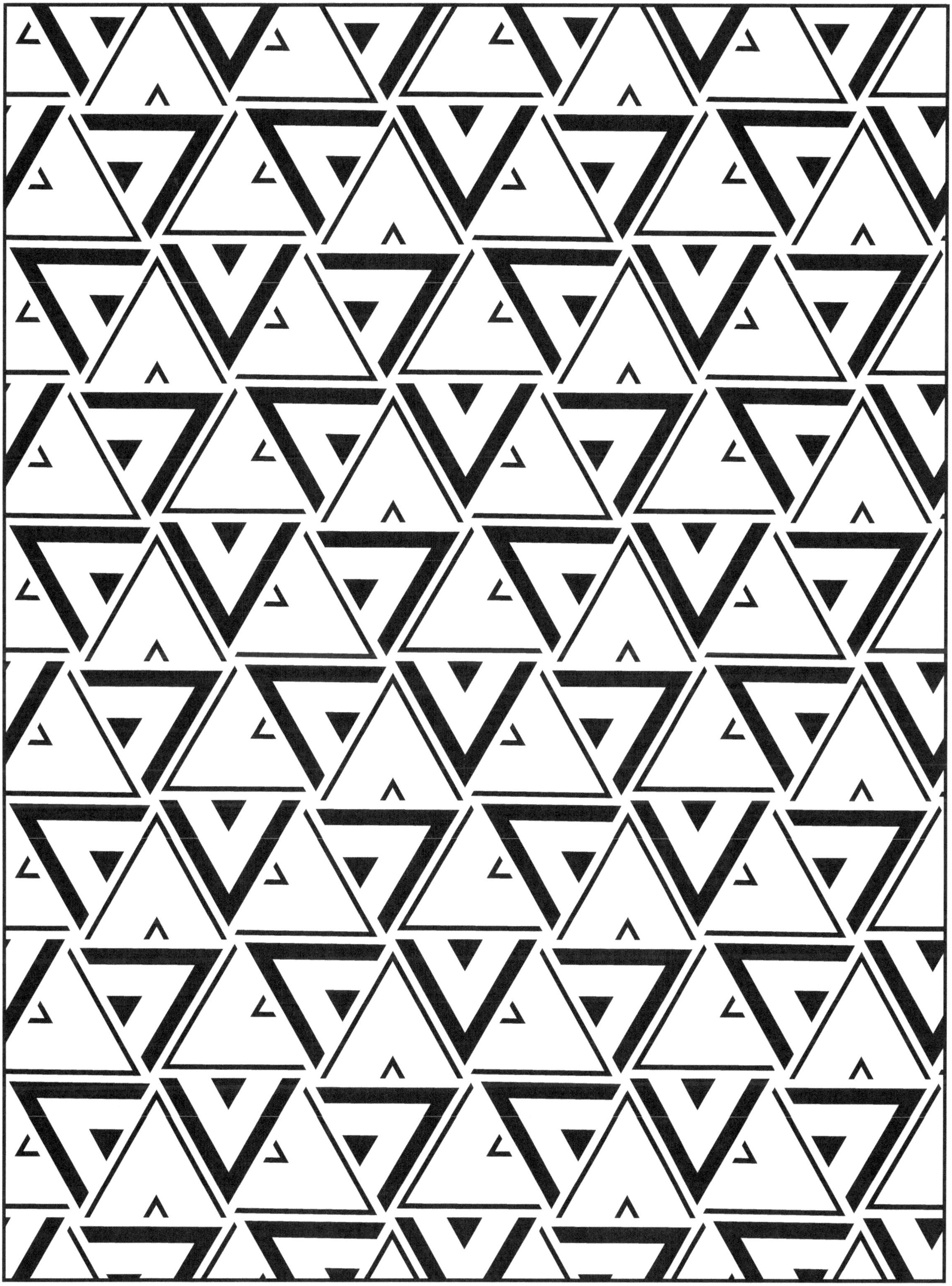

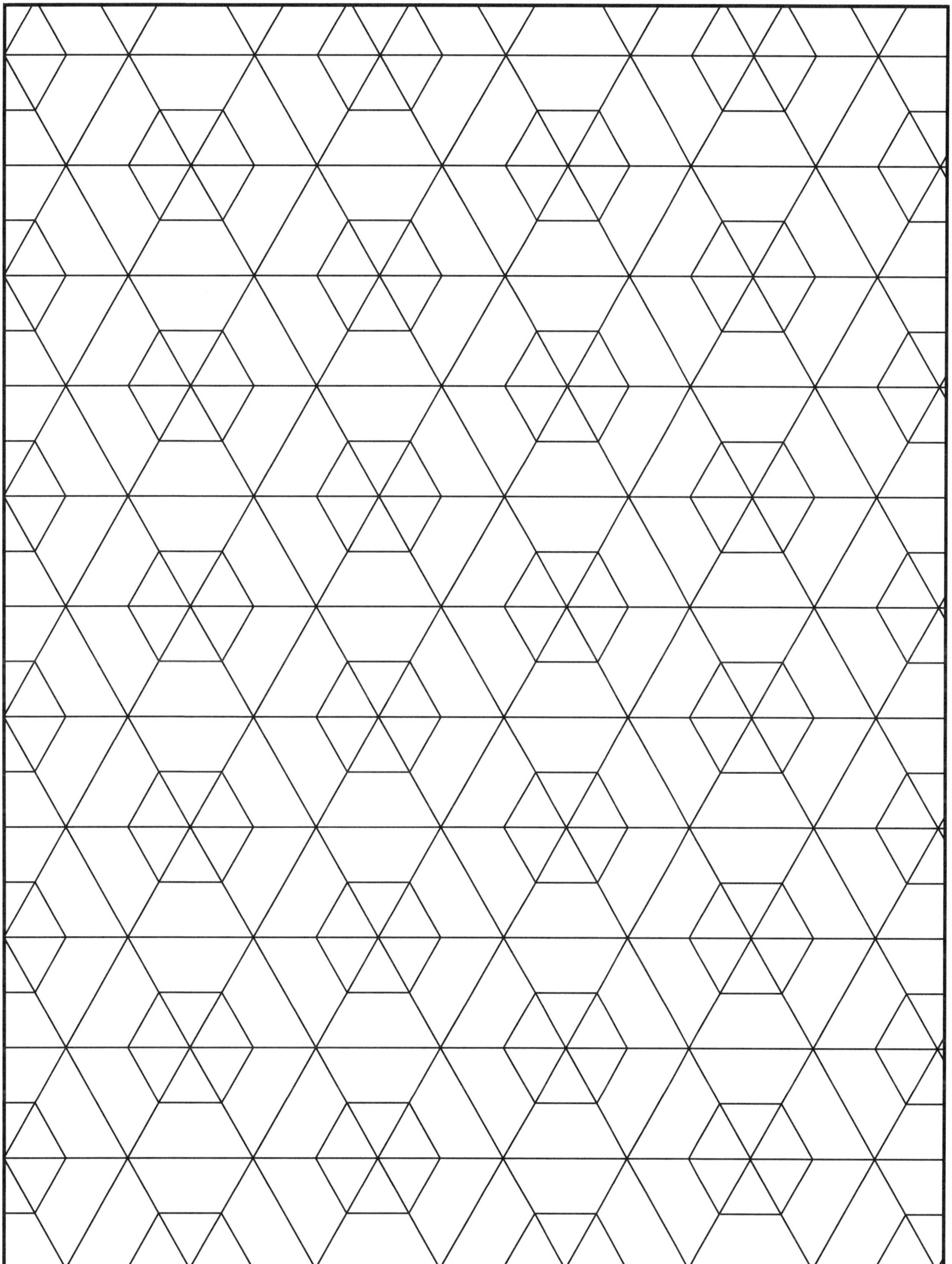

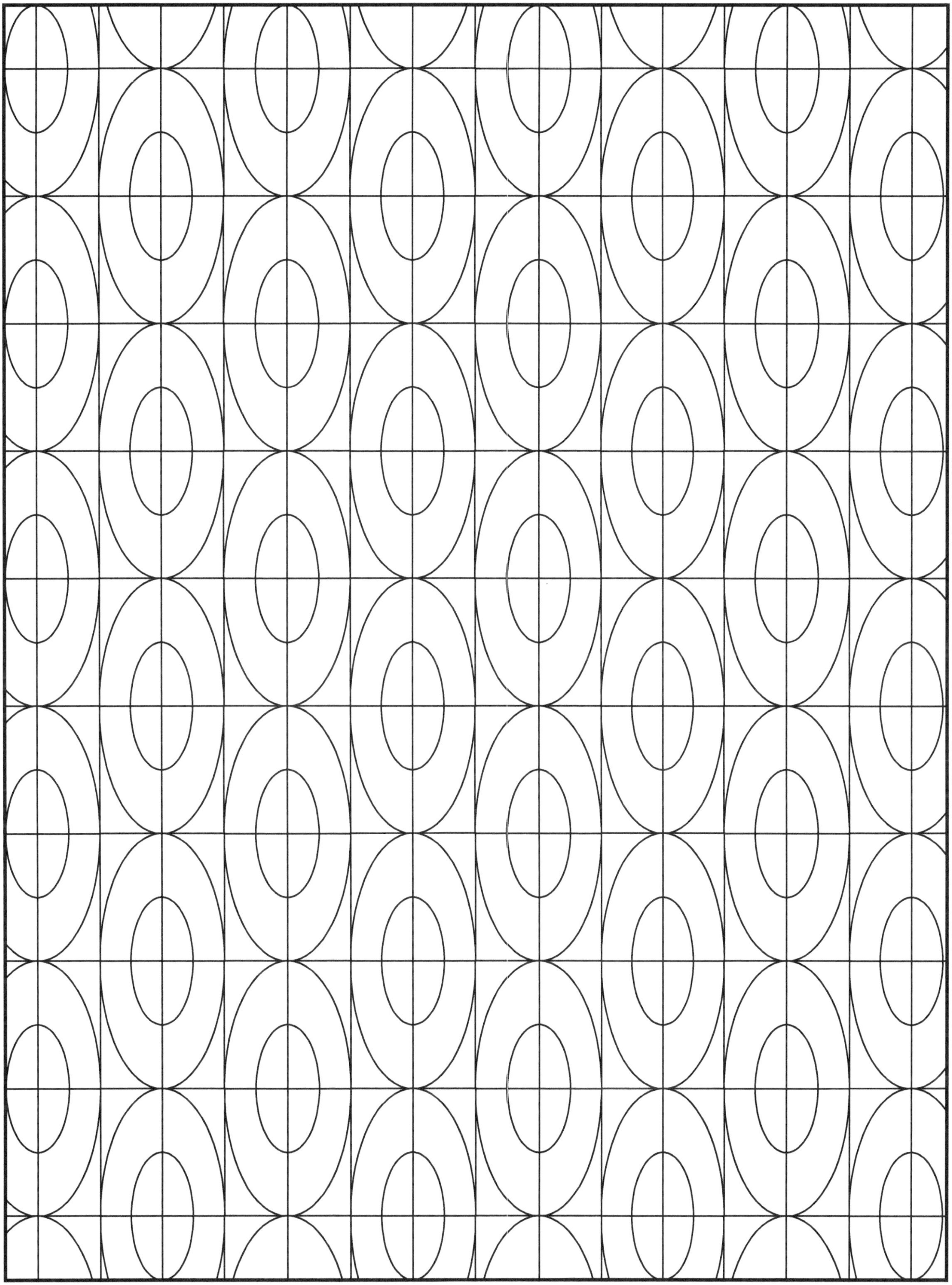

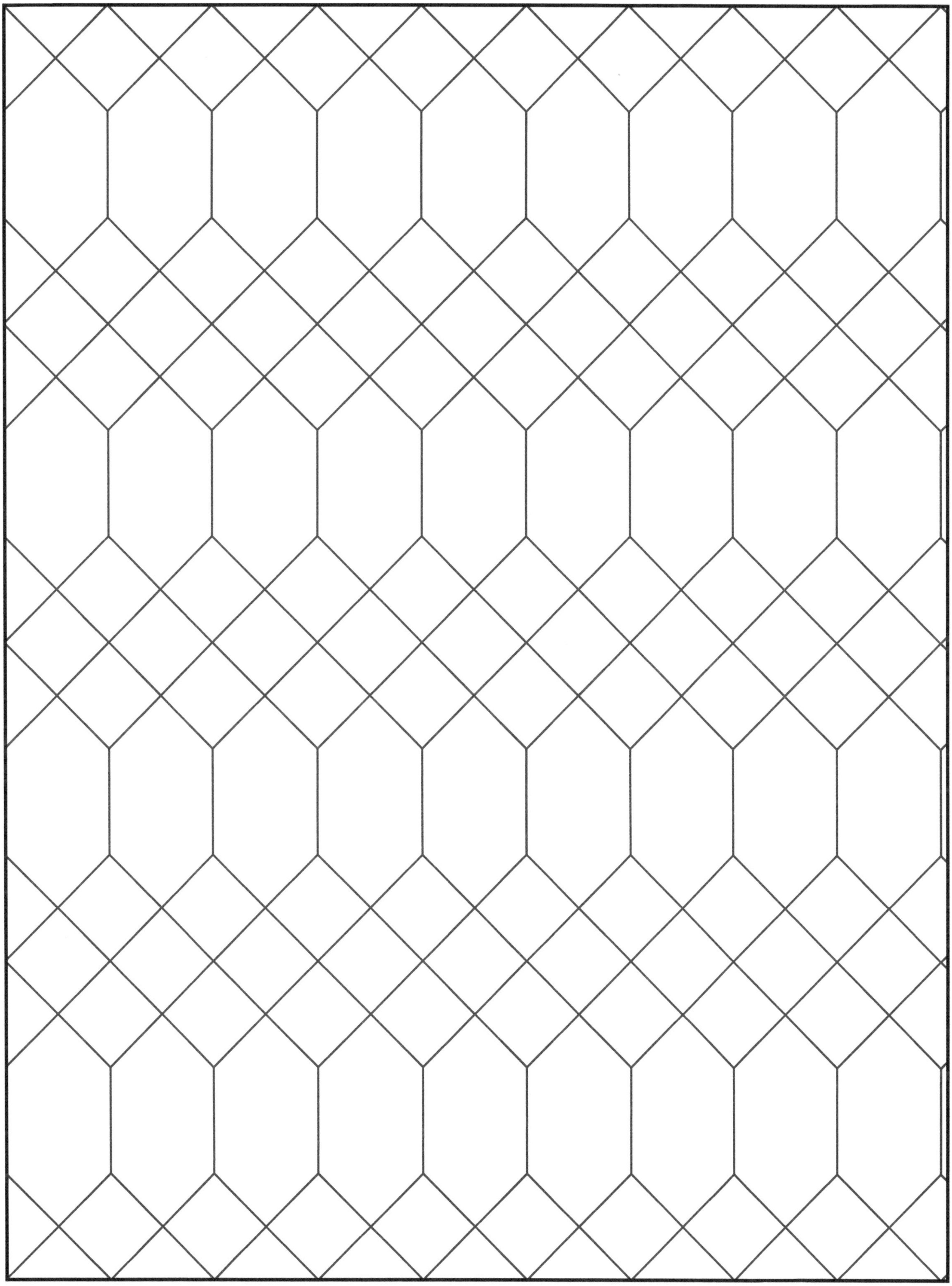

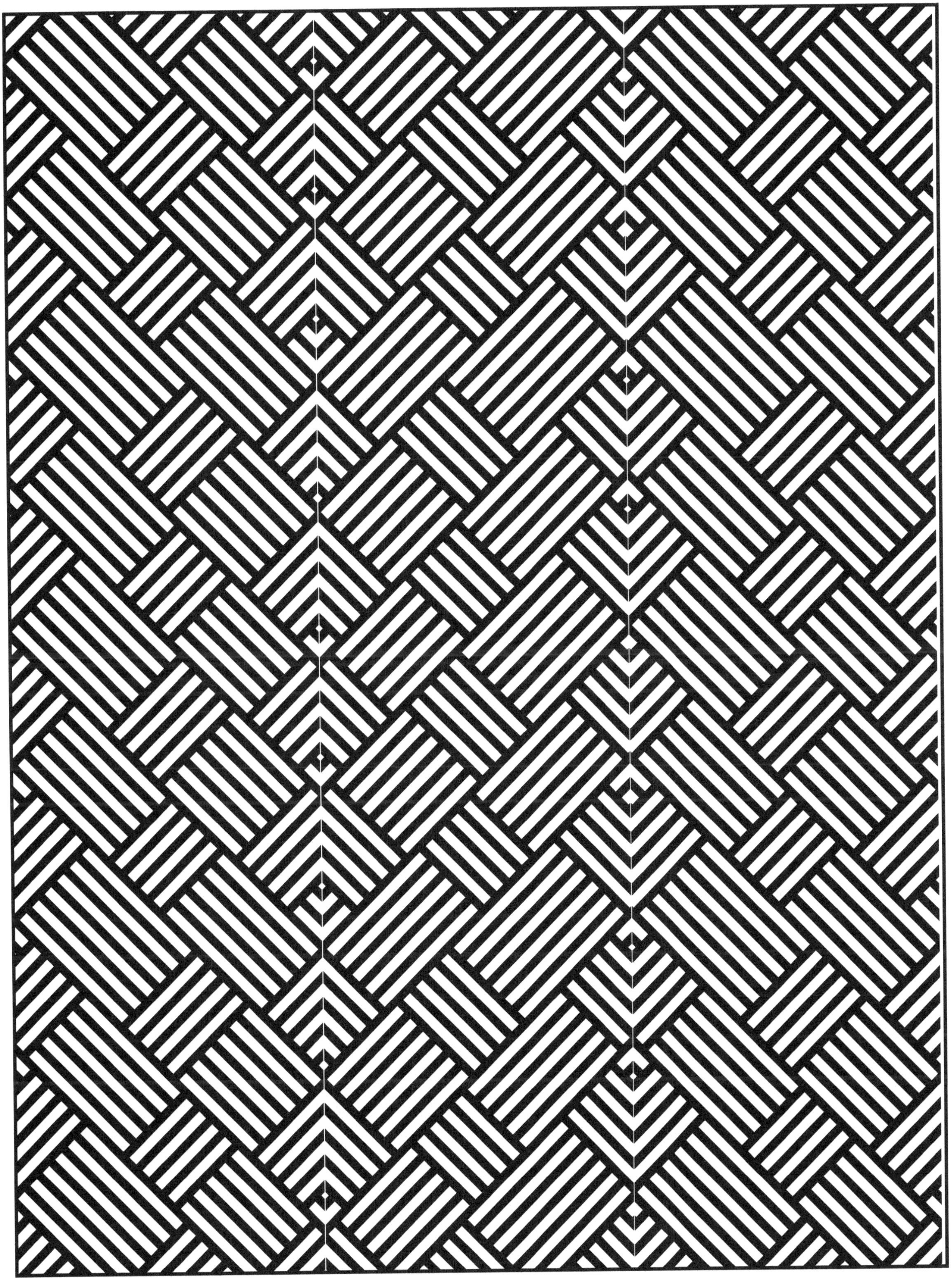

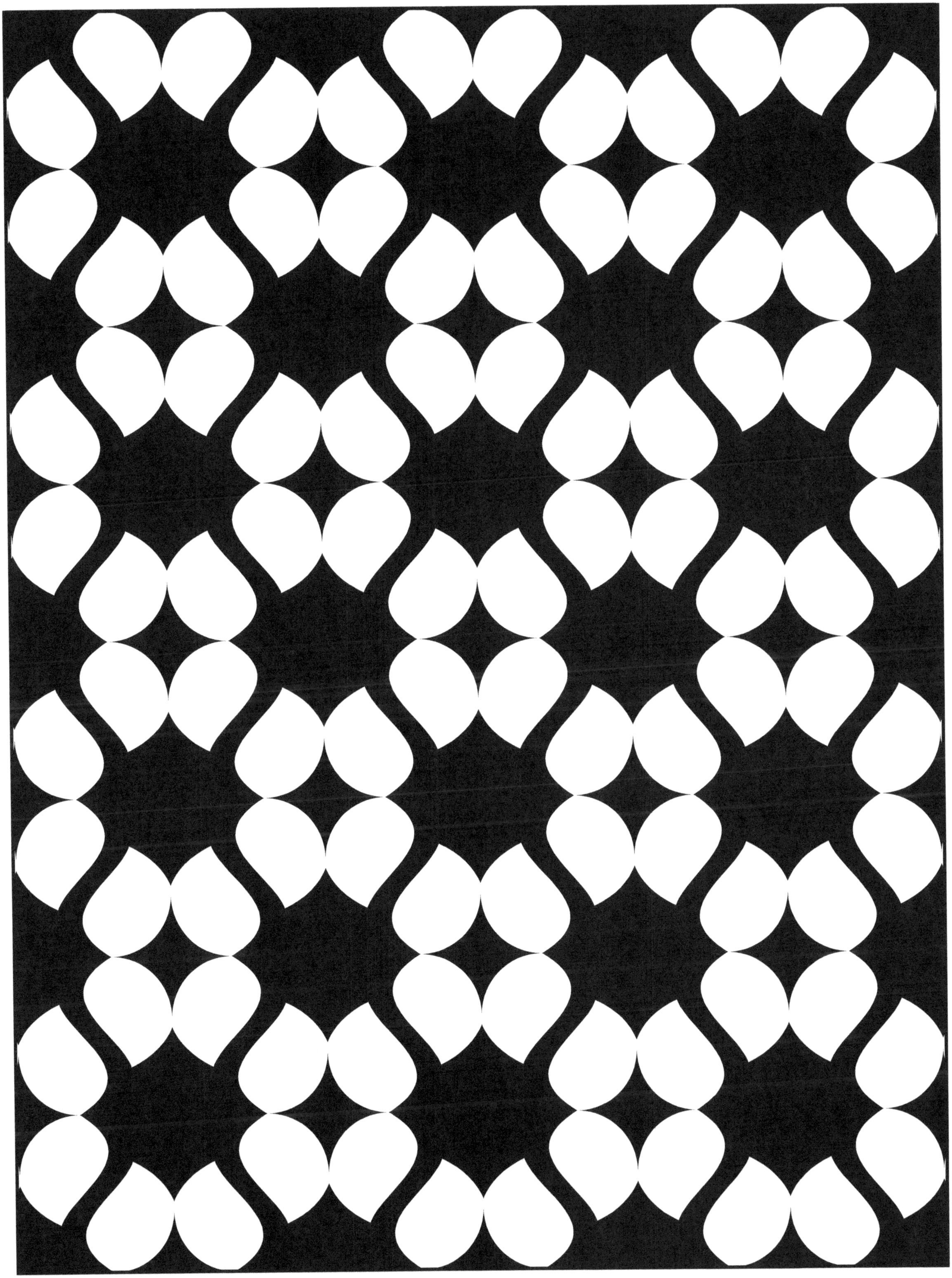

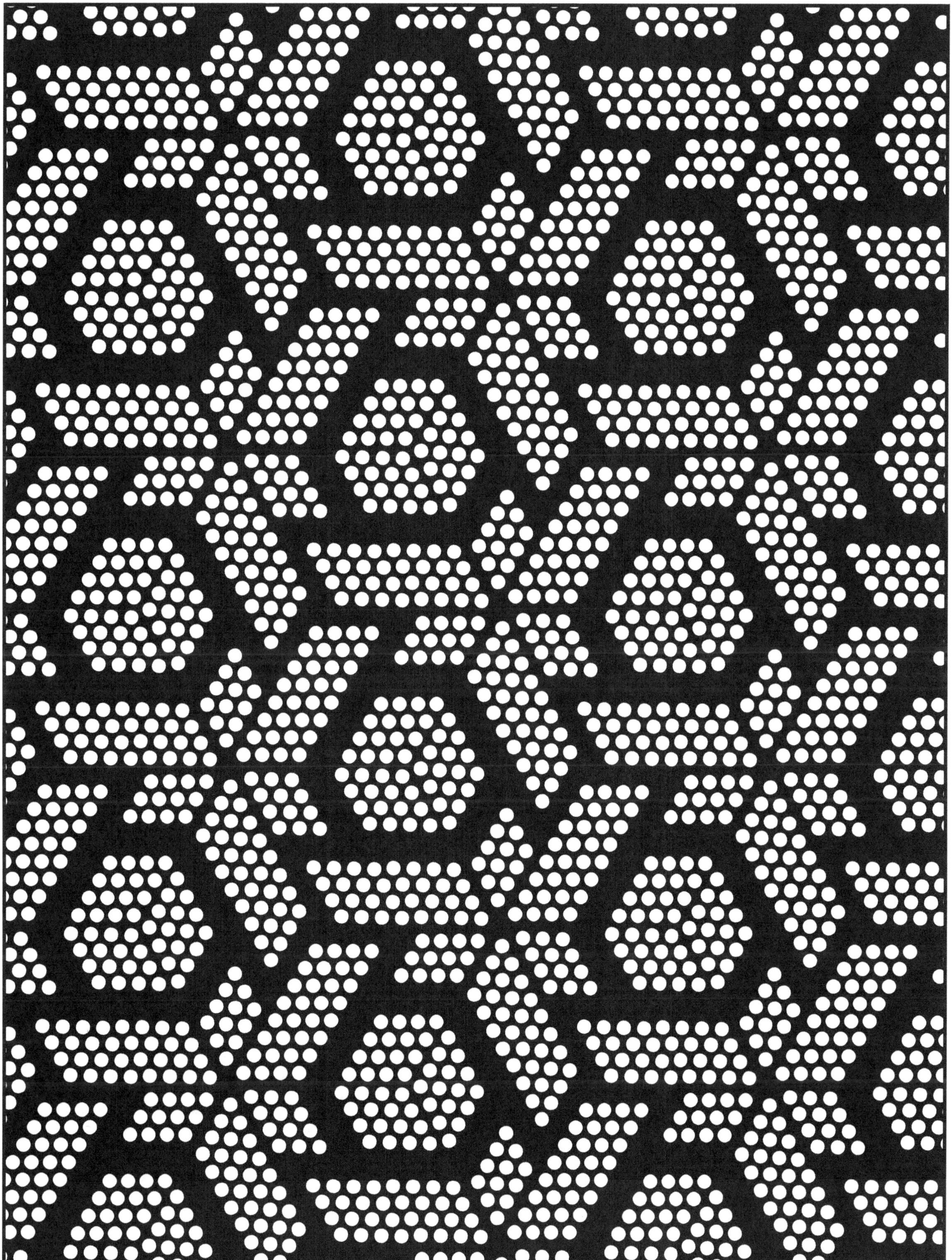

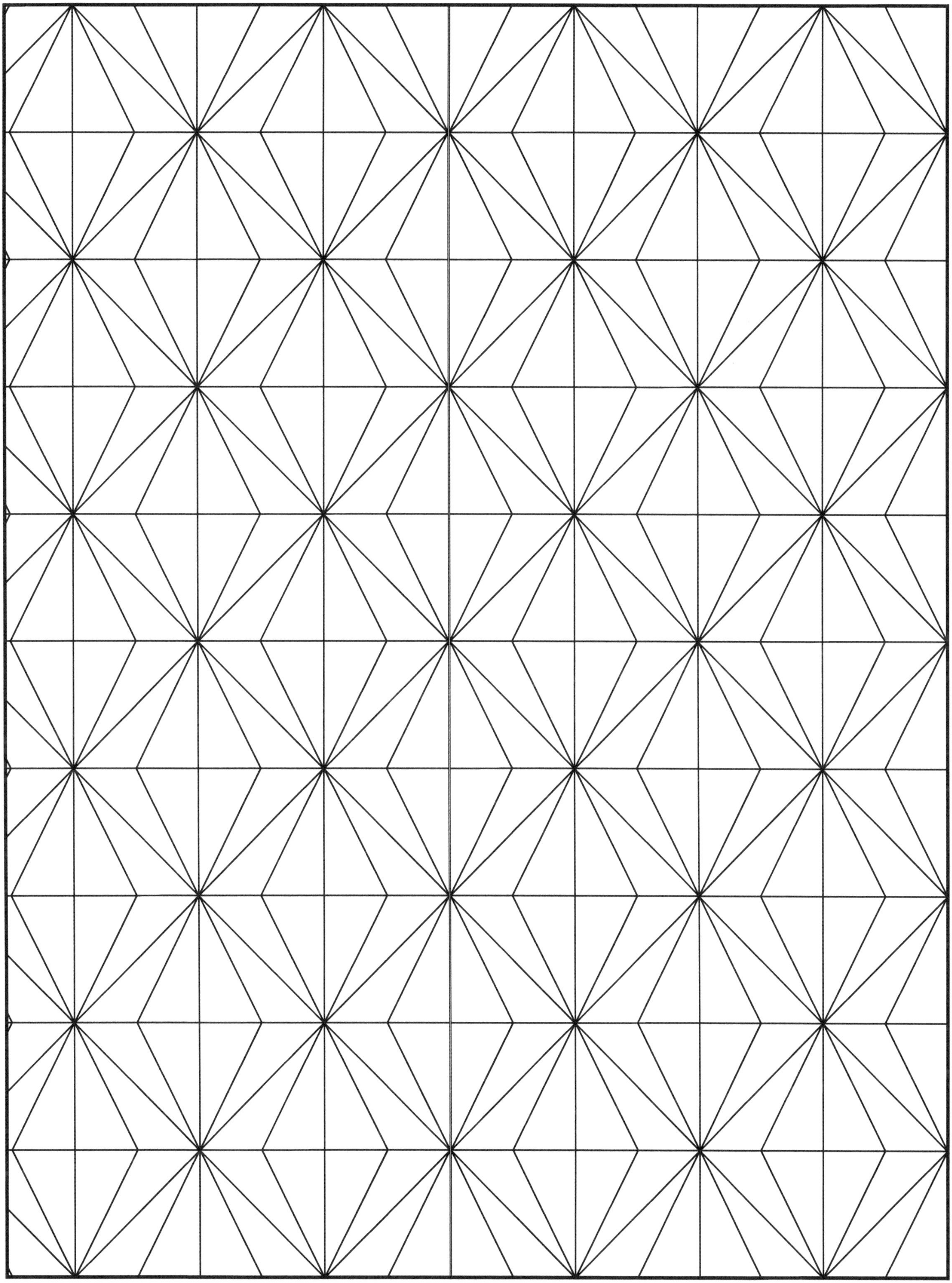

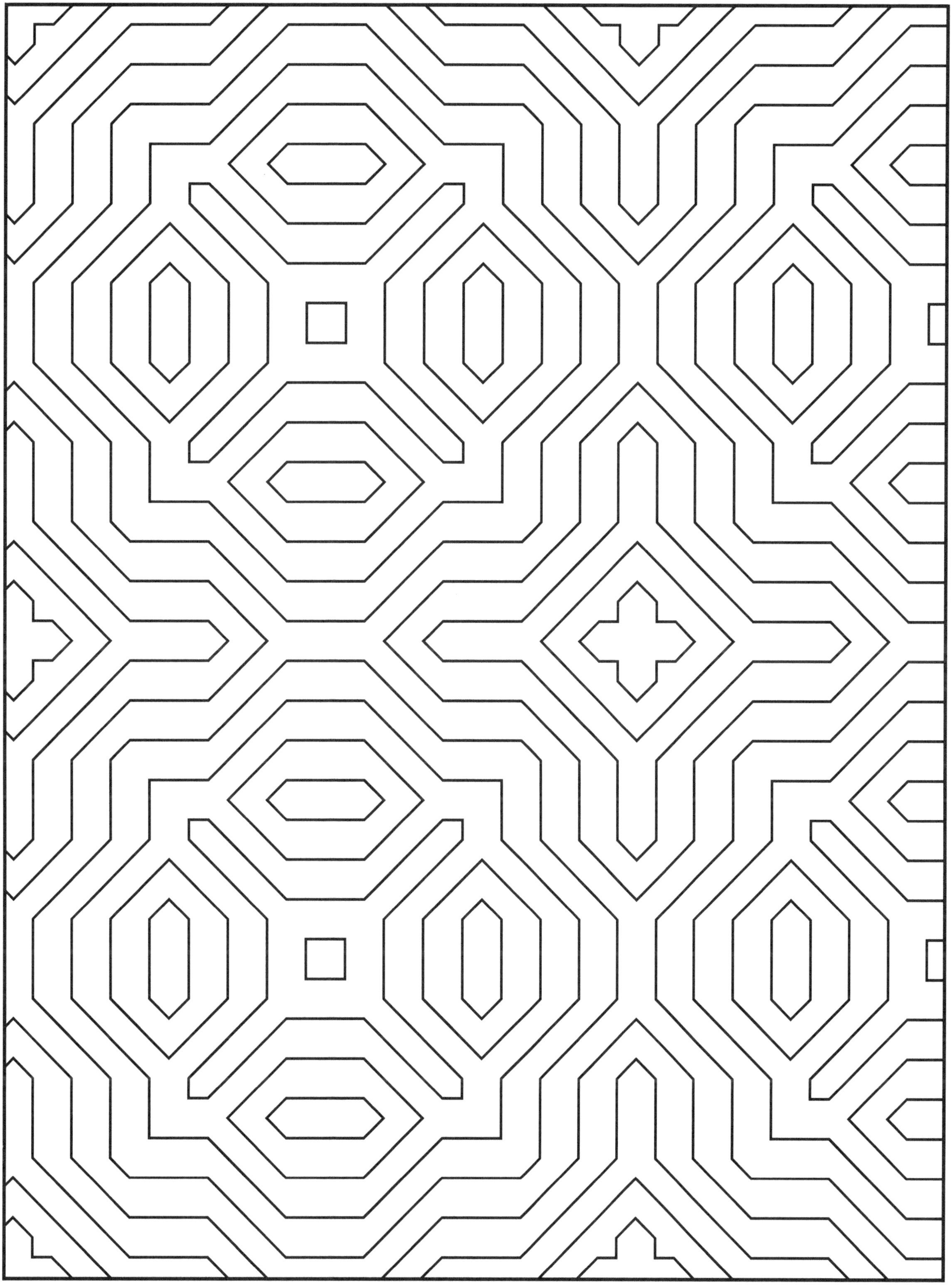

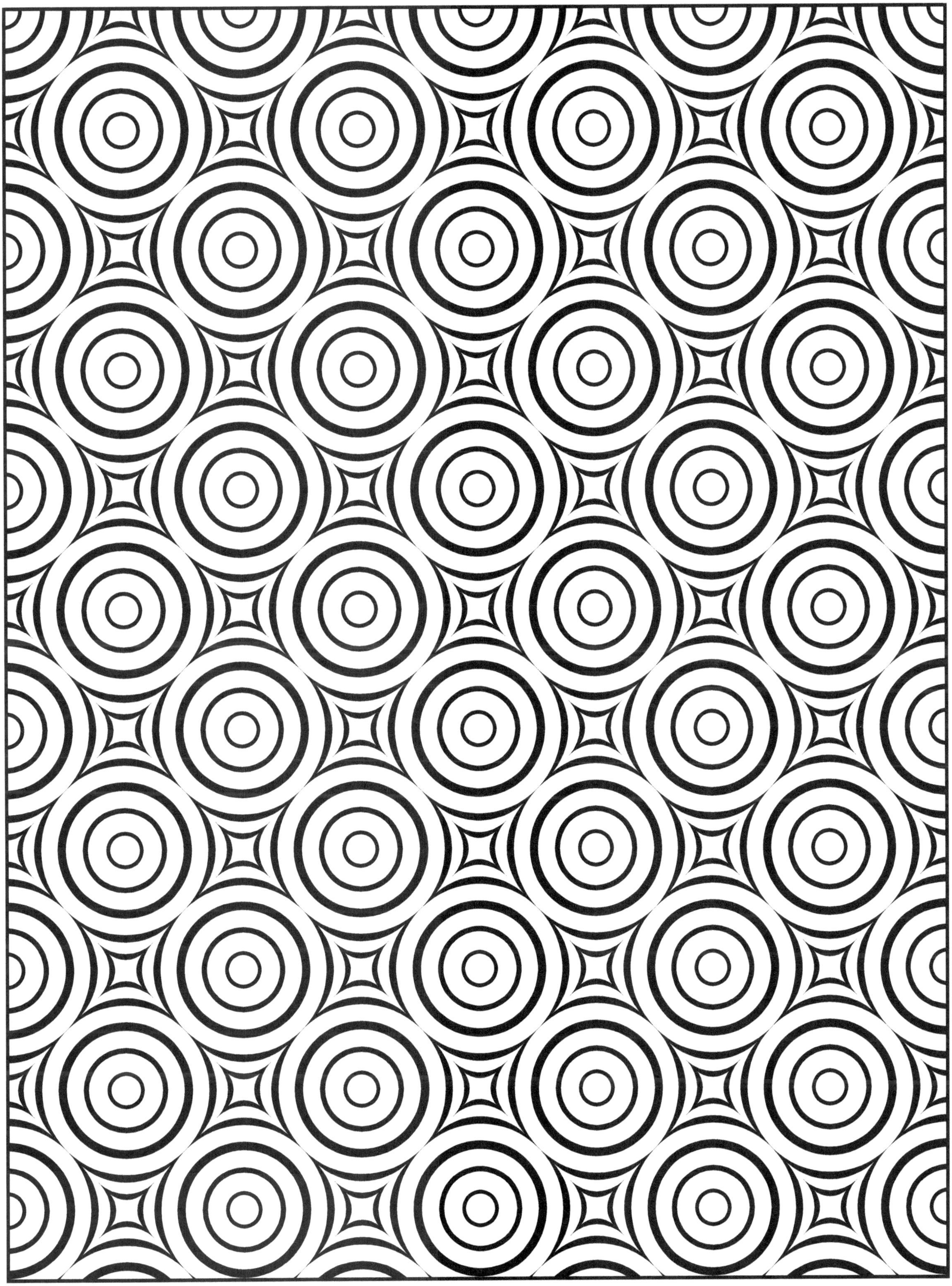

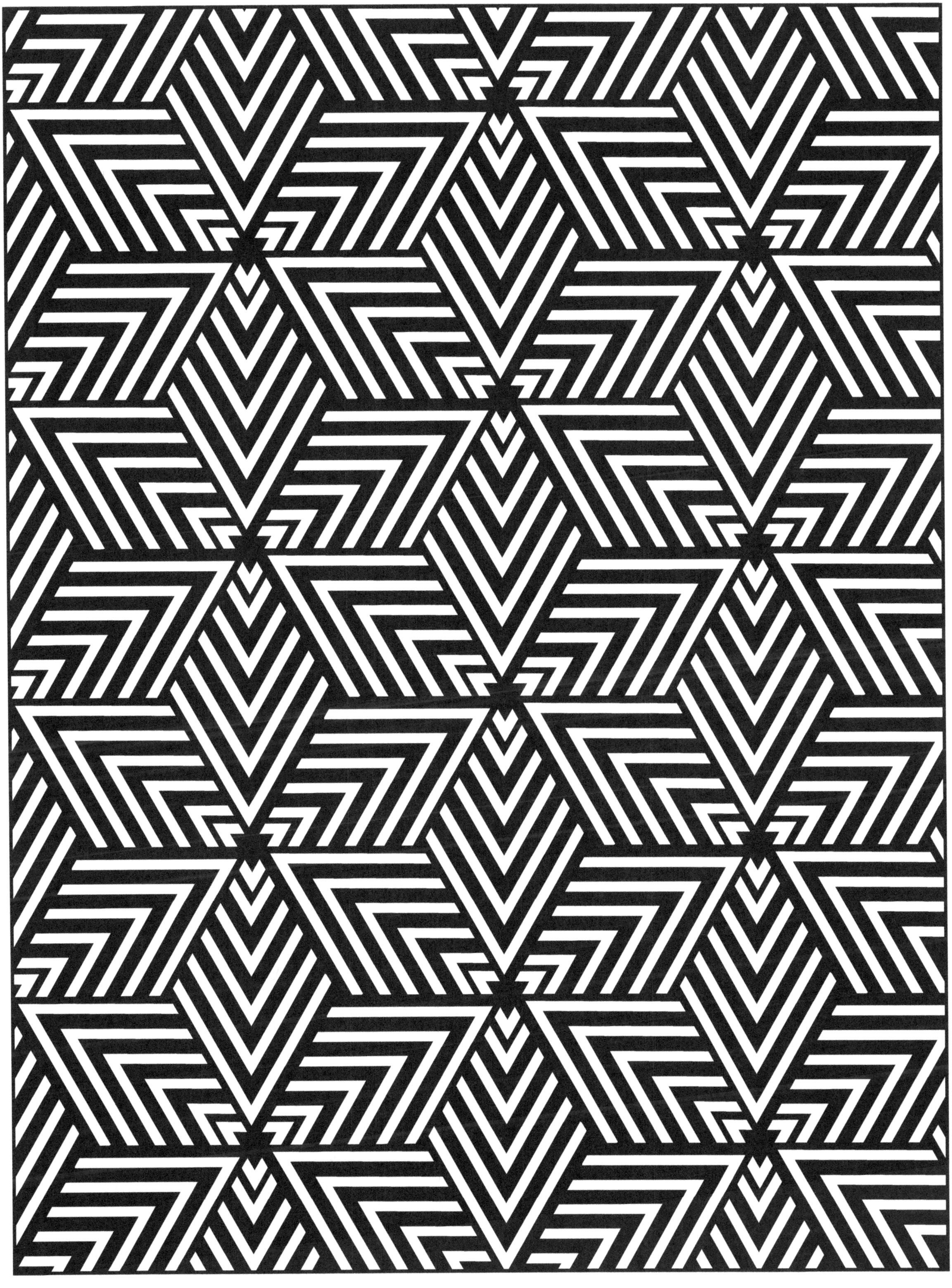

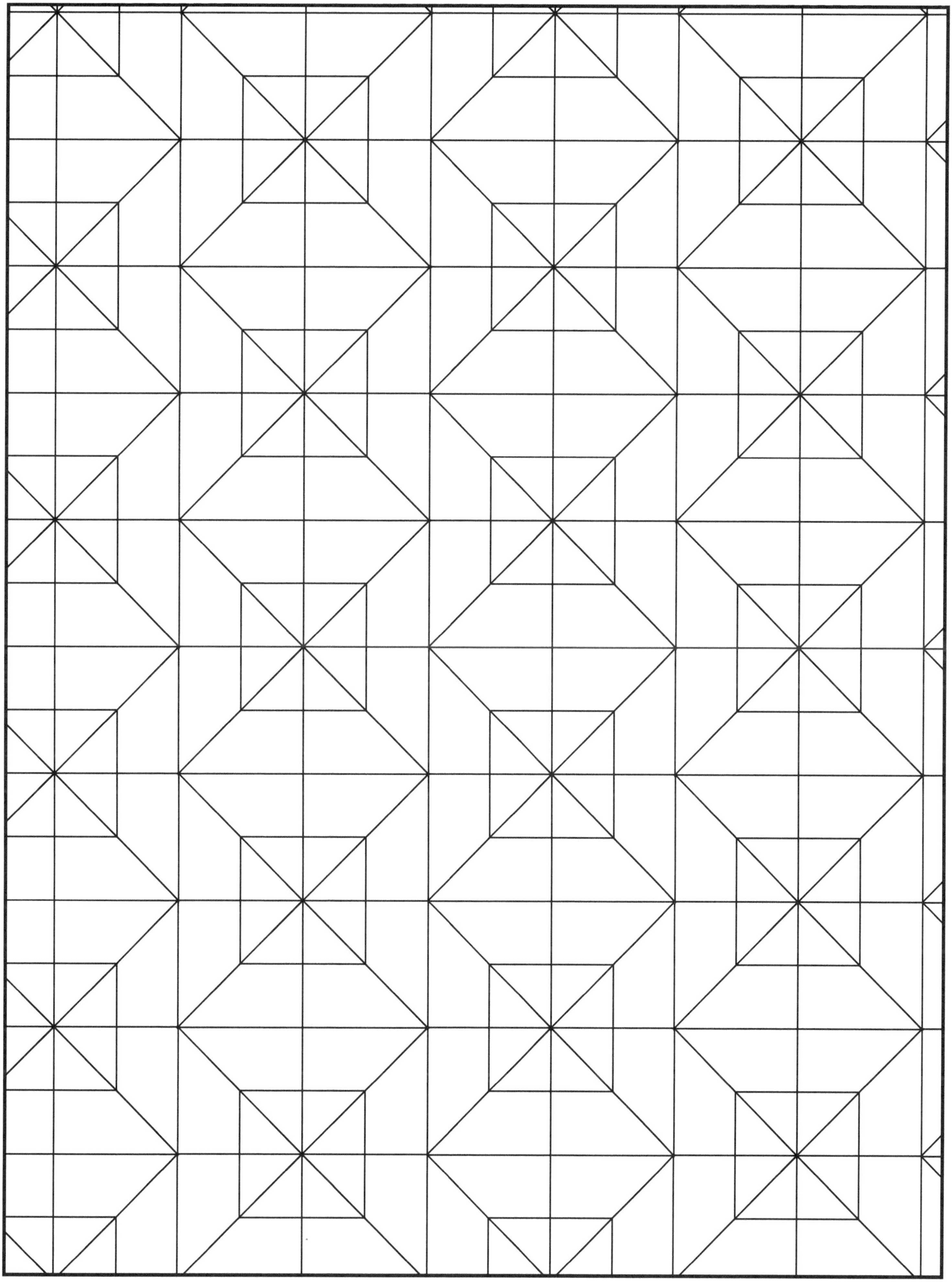

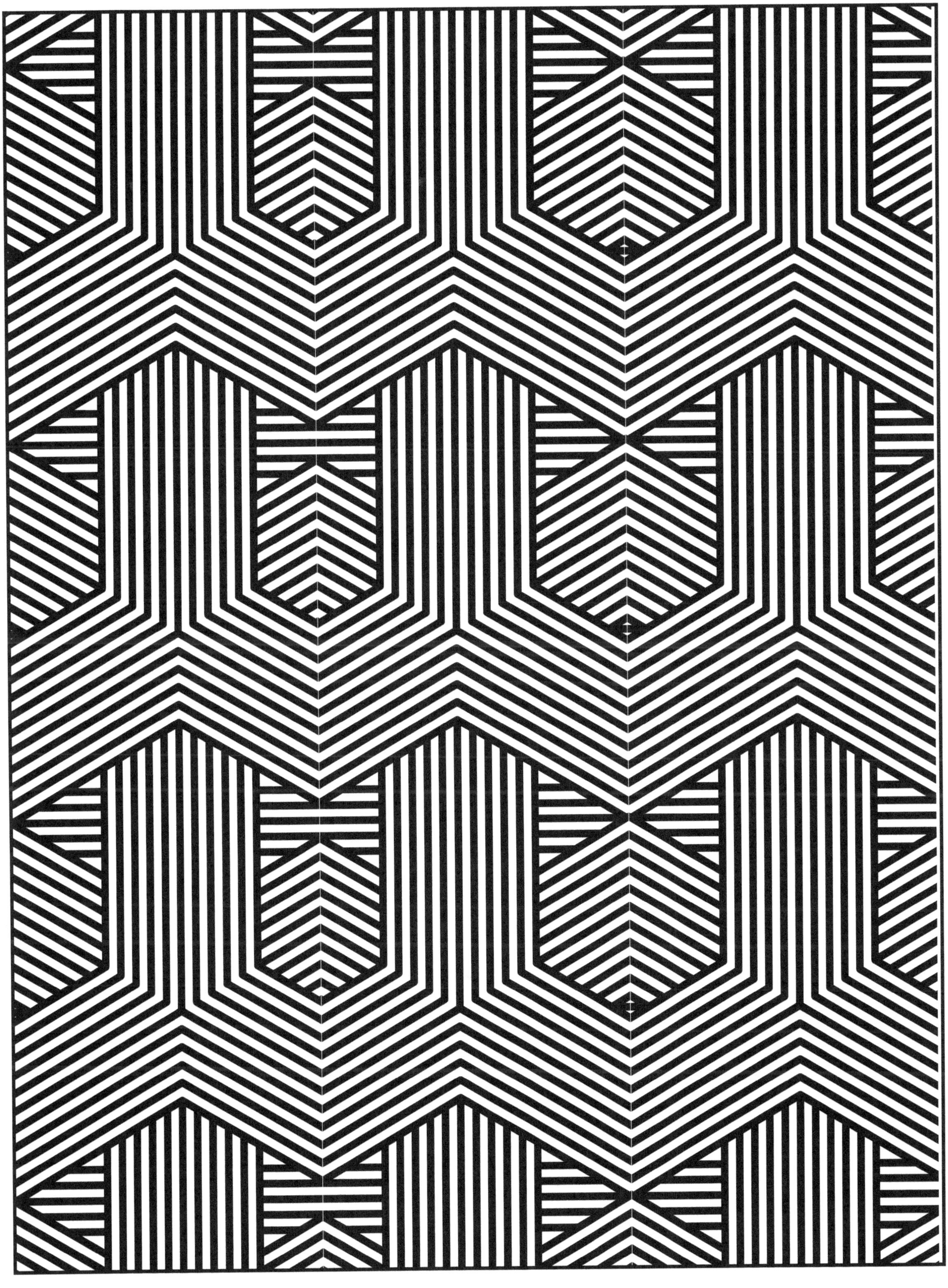

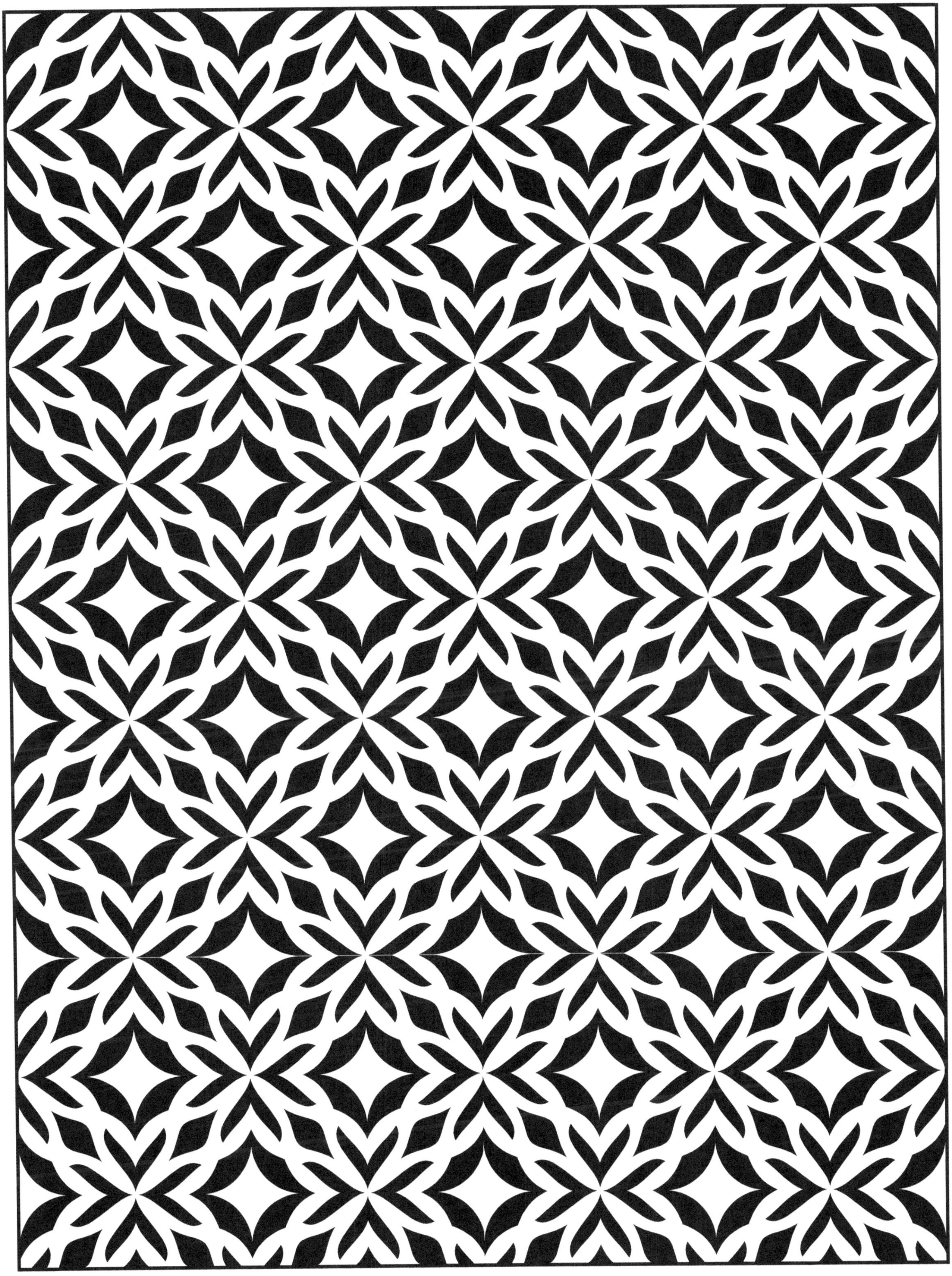

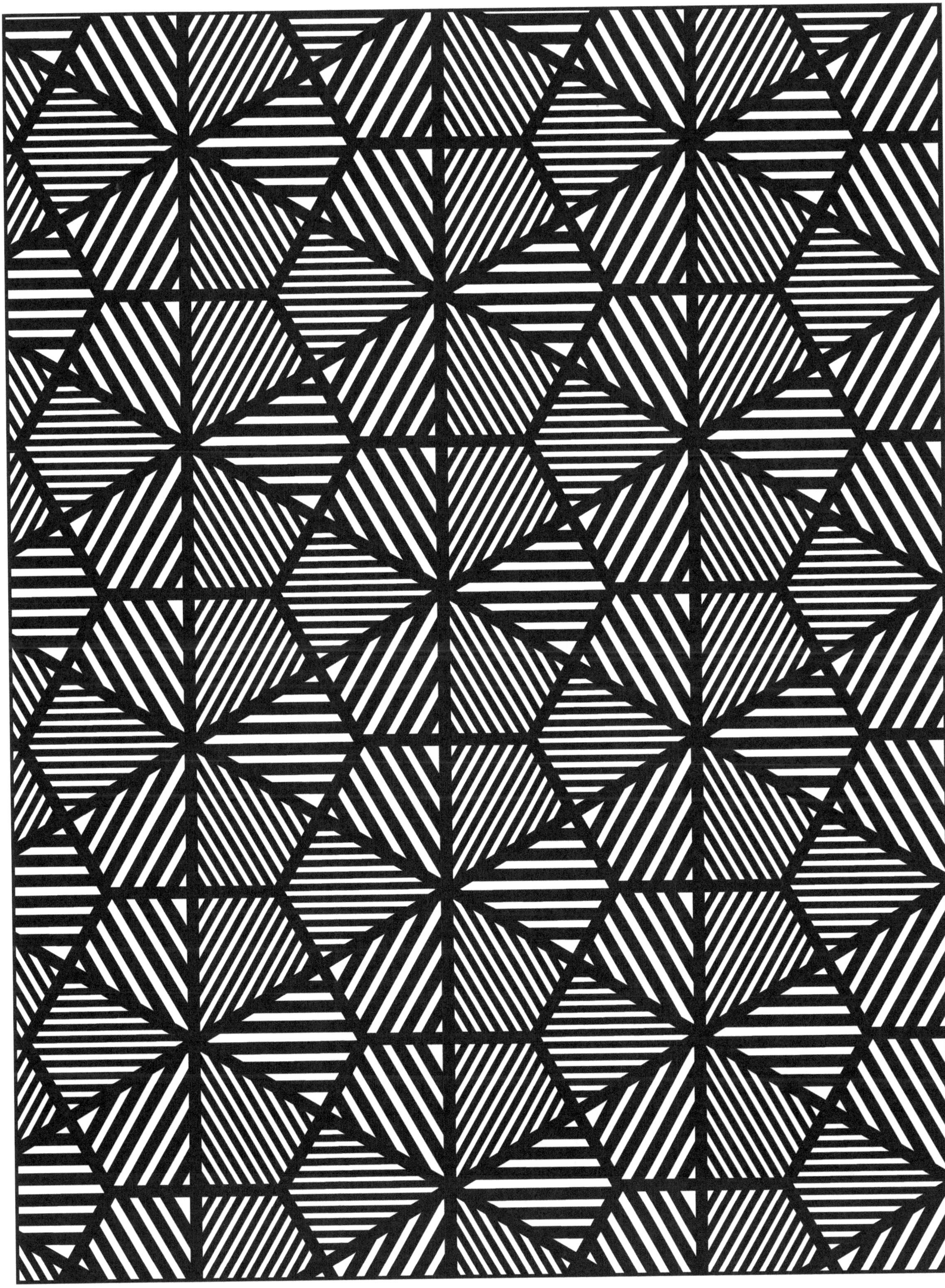

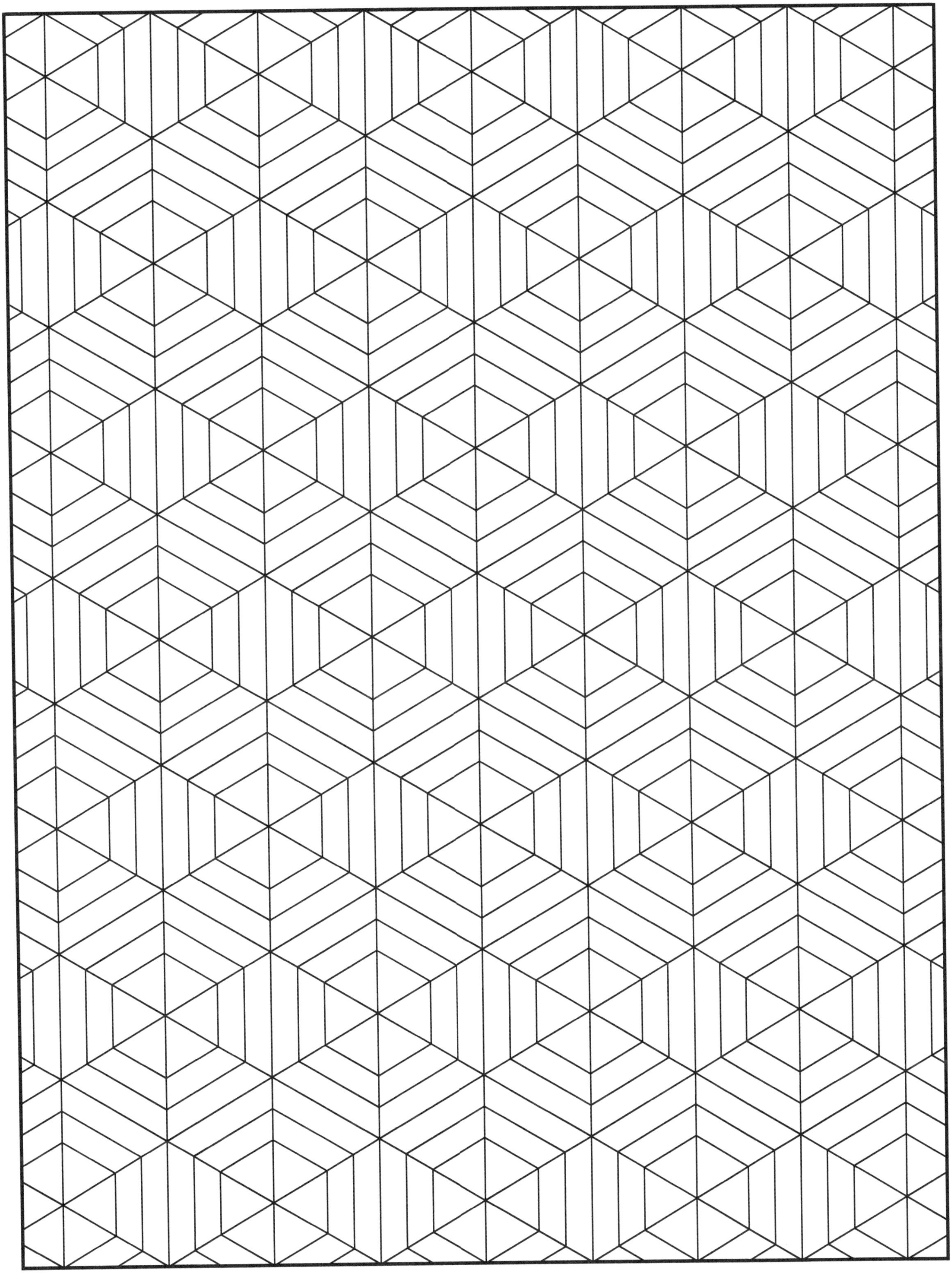

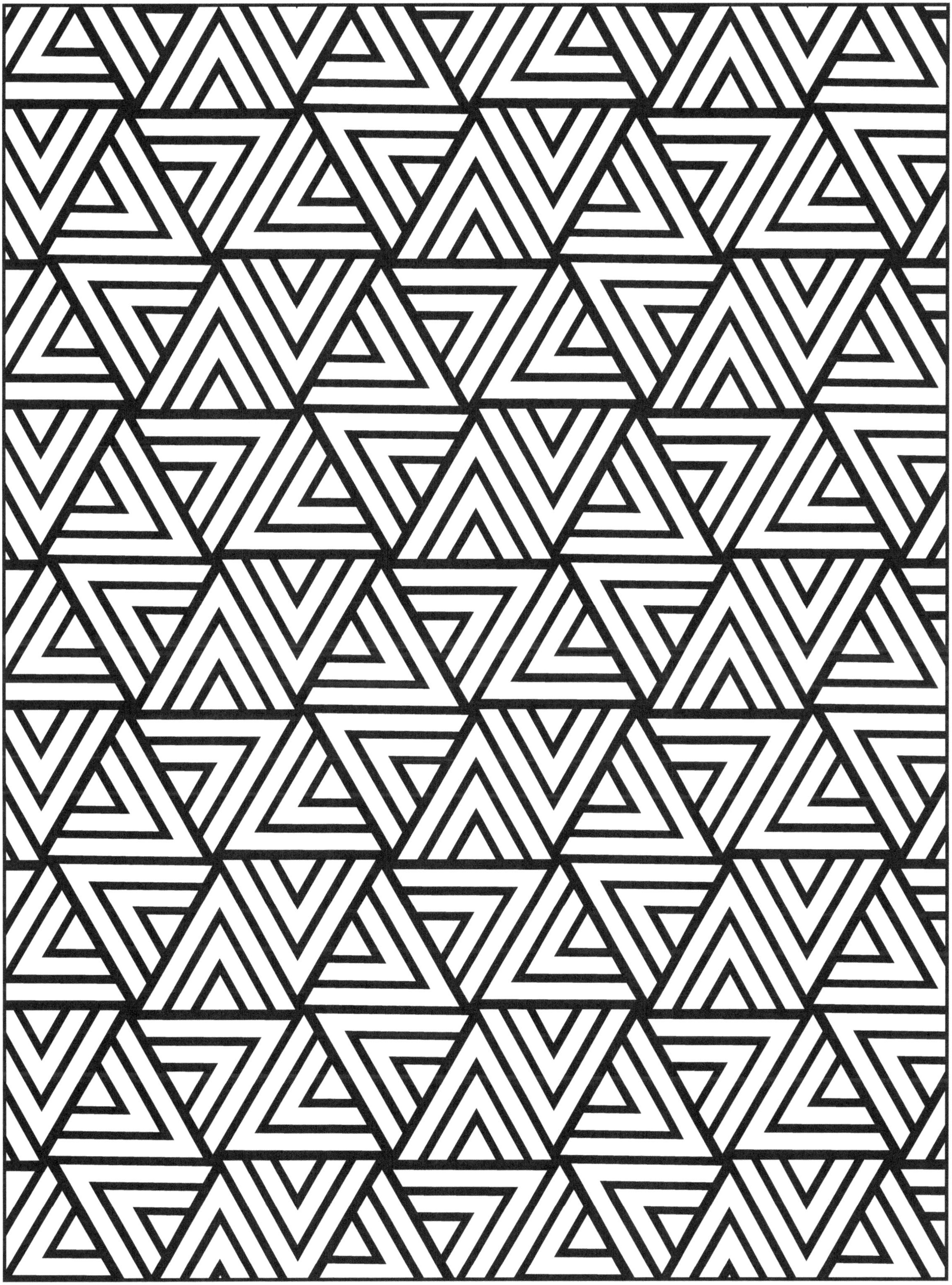

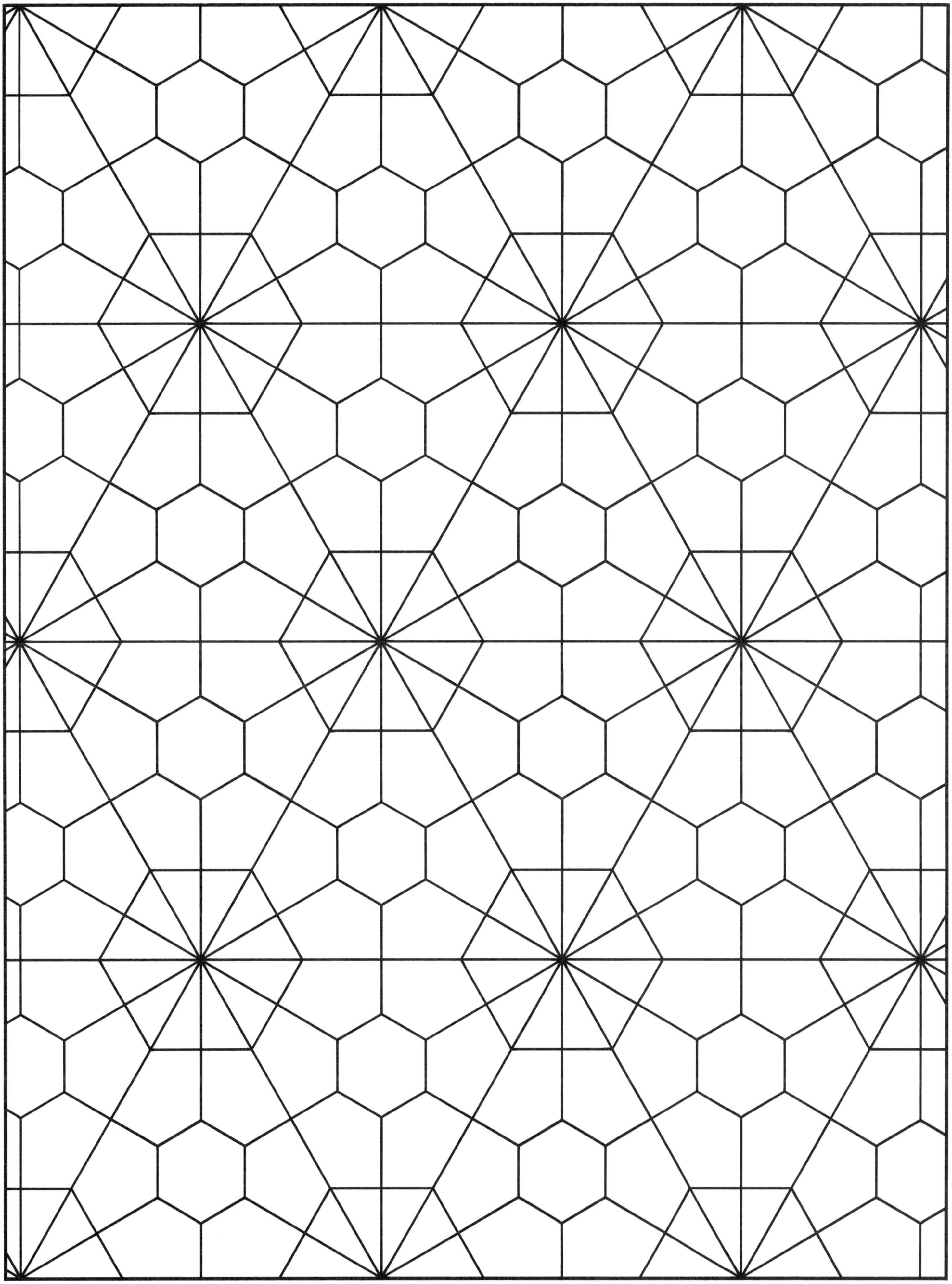

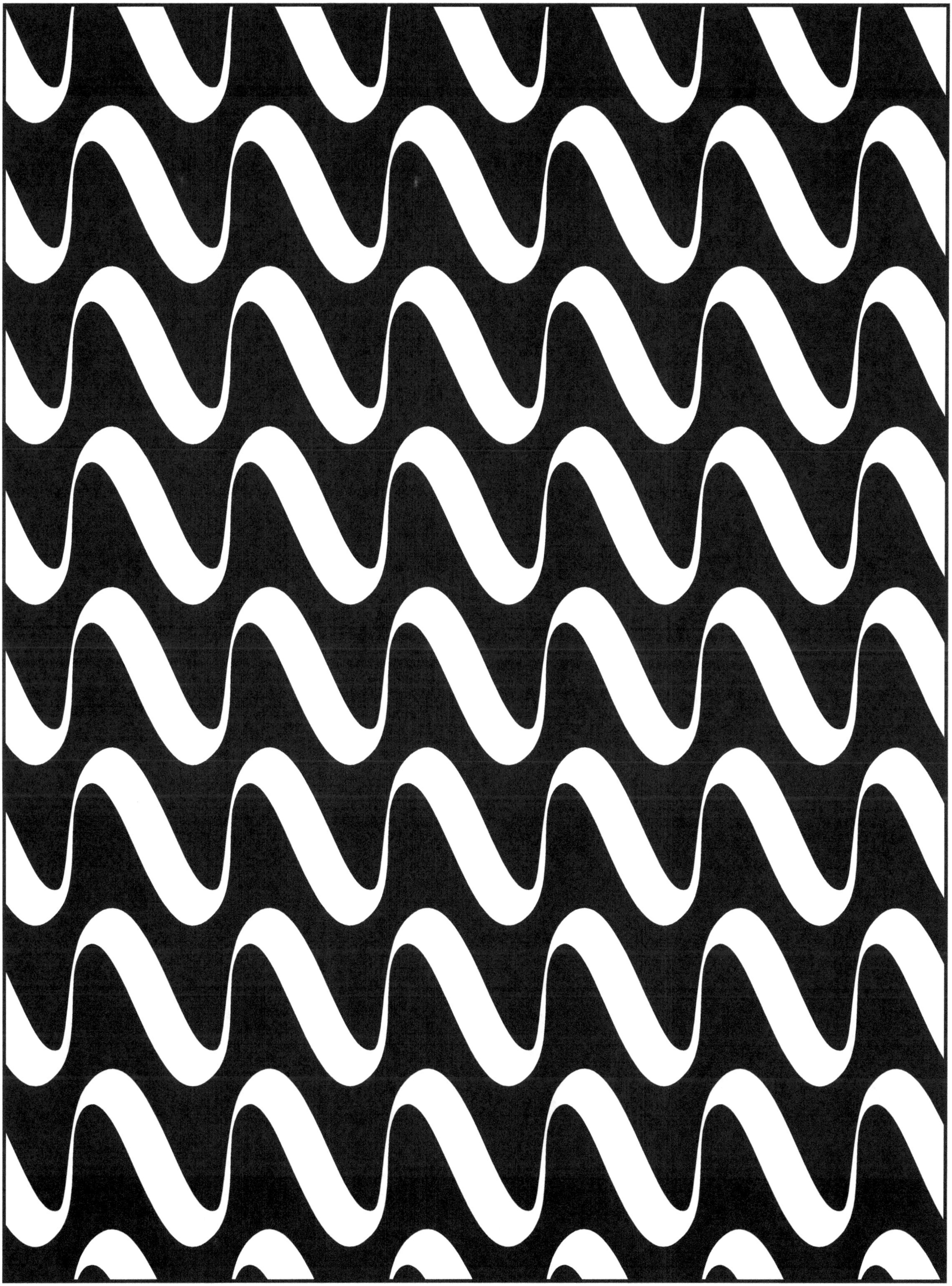

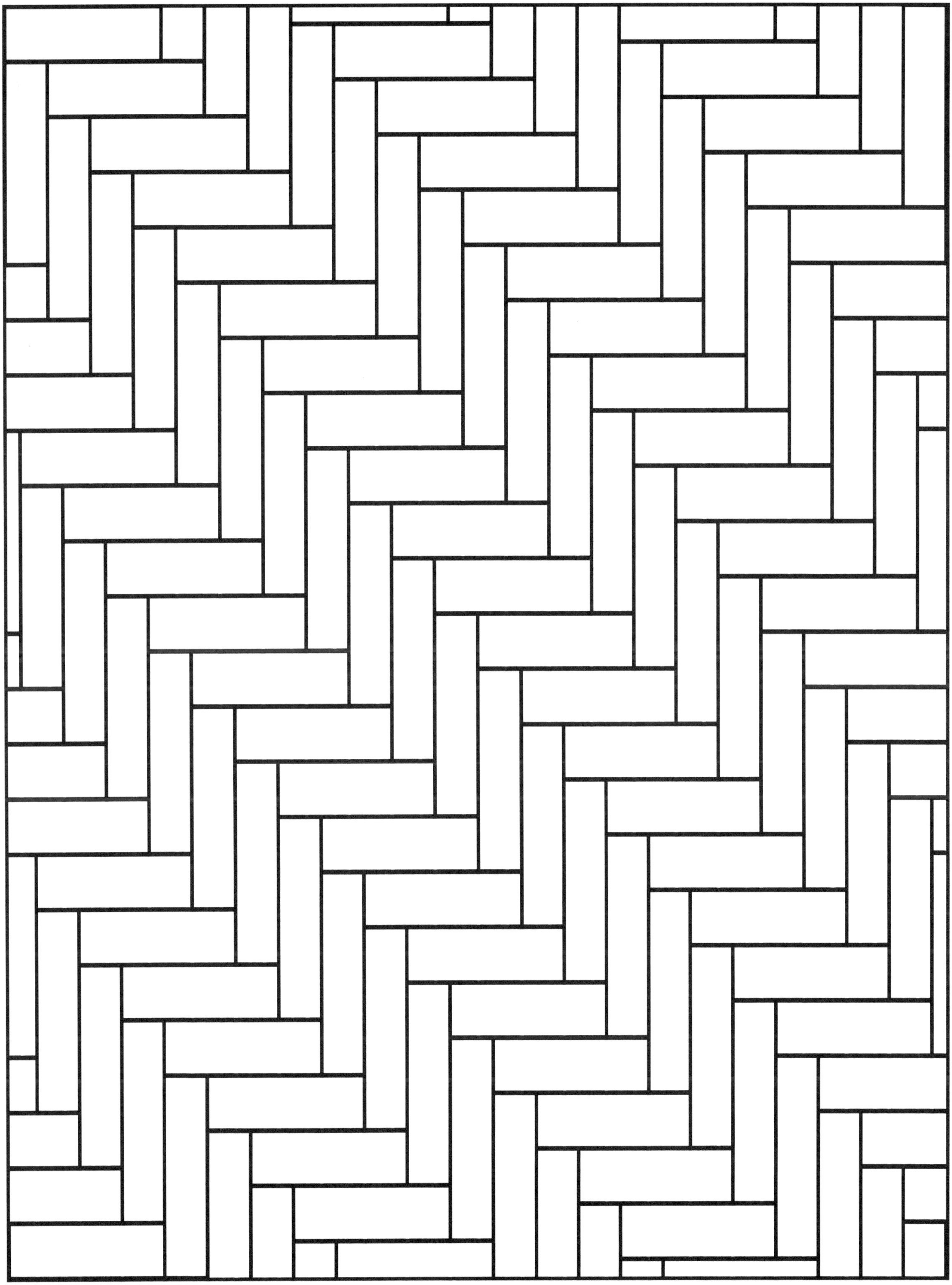

www.ingramcontent.com/pod-product-compliance
Lightning Source LLC
Chambersburg PA
CBHW062330220526
45469CB00008B/2656